LEADERSHIP

VOLUME 2

TORKOM SARAYDARIAN

LEADERSHIP SERIES

Contents

    Foreword 5
1. Leadership and God 9
2. Leader and Love 17
3. The Leader Faces Himself 21
4. Personality and Leadership 23
5. Leadership Tests 27
6. Leadership and Growth of Personality 31
7. Employees and Leader 35
8. Checking the Work 39
9. Leader to Be 41
10. Experience 45
11. Guidelines for Organizing a
      Correspondence Course 51
12. The Formulations of Law 63
13. Leadership and the Law of Repulsion 69
14. Leaders and Crystallizations 81
15. Leadership and Confusion 87
16. Vigilance 105
17. World Leadership 113
18. Self-Confidence 129
19. Toward Greatness 137
20. Leadership and Miracles 147
21. Leadership and Renunciation 153

22. Practical Suggestions 157
23. Leadership and the Mystery of Manifestation 169
24. Ever-Moving Forward 175
25. Forgiveness 183
26. Losing Faith 193
27. How to Work 199
28. Laws of Life 203
29. The Three Enemies of the Leader-to-Be 211
30. Leadership and Warnings 215
31. Writing Letters 225
32. Leadership Defined 231
33. Leadership and Ideas 235
34. Leadership and Motives 241
35. A Few Practical Steps for Leaders 247
36. Rules for Telephone Conversations 265
37. Studying Both Sides 271
38. Leadership and Co-Workers 275
39. The Center and the Circle 281
40. Lecturing 287
41. Right Use of Time 295
42. Fear 301
43. Leadership and Treason 305
    Index 311
    Bibliographic References 327

Foreword

The Leadership Series is a series of books on the subject of leadership defined for the New Era, the Future. These books are written to evoke the leadership qualities in every human being in all fields of life. Whether you are the leader of a large corporation or the leader of a small group of people, the principles and guidelines given in this series will be of tremendous help in your daily professional and personal activities. The principles outlined in these books are timeless and relate to the core values of the human experience. All great leaders in all fields of life have demonstrated these core principles.

In all departments of human labor, there is a need for leaders who have vision, initiative, determination, vitality, and enthusiasm. There is a need for leaders who are able to stand against limitation of movement, ignorance, disorderliness, and ugliness. There is a need for leaders who are equipped with knowledge in their field of labor and who are equipped with the wisdom to protect their field of labor and their co-workers. There is a need for leaders who understand core values and principles and stand on them regardless of the common practices to the contrary.

The ideas given on leadership in these series of books are taken from a lifetime of experience in leadership. They cover every area of leadership. These ideas can be applied in any field. The principles are the same; a true leader can learn from one field and apply his learning to any other field.

Leadership is

- example
- sacrifice
- wisdom
- daring
- fearlessness
- nobility
- humility
- gratitude
- courage

Any leader in any field needs these principles.

Leadership is the answer of a need and it is the future. On one hand, the leader responds to the need; on the other hand, he is the leader of the future.

In any field a leader must respond to the need as well as carry out his labor in order to meet the needs of the future.

If the reader thinks that I am referring to a leader of a particular field in these series of books, he must know that he is hindering his vision.

Leadership is not gender specific, nor is it specific to any field. It is not specific to a particular form of dress, physical characteristics, or ways of behavior. Leadership in its essence is based on deep inner values and a commitment to the advancement and continuous growth of others. A true leader is a spiritual teacher and is found in every field of life such as science, religion, politics, arts, and business. The spiritual teacher does not mean a religious teacher, but a person who ever seeks new ways of approach, new fields of discovery, new levels of consciousness both for himself and others. In a sense, any leader equipped with such tendencies is a spiritual teacher and a leader.

A group in my mind is any aggregation of individuals who work for the Common Good. A real group can be formed only by conscious people whose orientation is to help each other, to help manifest great principles, and generally to serve the needs of all.

These series of books can be used by a corporate executive as well as a church priest, a parent, the individual who wants to lead himself out of limitations, as well as the teacher in a classroom.

One of the greatest abilities of a true leader is inclusiveness or synthesis. For him, each field of human endeavor is not a separate world but a department of the one field of life. A true leader can fit into any department in a very short time.

After you study these series of books, you will be able to see how true leadership is inspired and directed by great principles and values in all fields of life. We hope that the leader existing in you may be evoked and you too will take the responsibility of leadership.

These pages carry my experiences of forty years. I give them to those who can use them in their self-sacrificial service for the entire humanity. Most of these chapters were used as study papers for a selected number of students.

Here then is *Leadership*, Volume Two.

Torkom Saraydarian

1996

1
Leadership and God

Leadership is learned when the human being finds a reason to bring his personality into line with higher principles or the standards of Higher Worlds.

Each time the human being is able to improve his physical, emotional, and mental life and introduces higher direction in them toward the future, toward the service of humanity, he learns the secrets of leadership.

The personality vehicles reflect exactly the three types of men who need leadership — the materialistic man, the man lost in his emotions, the man who is trapped in his mental modifications. In learning how to lead his personality, he learns to lead these three types of men which form the majority of the people.

Before a man is put in a high position, he must be sure that he is trained as a leader of his personality. Before one can lead his personality he cannot lead people who are formed by these kinds of personalities.

If the leadership toward his personality is weak, and he tries to lead people, his leadership will be a weak leadership — full of failures and defeats, corresponding exactly to the level of his personality leadership.

Many leaders witness this very sincerely: that failures within themselves are just like the failures in their field of service. If they correct their leadership of their personality, then leadership in the field of their service will be corrected and improved. The motivation and success of leadership rest upon the leadership carried on in the field of their personality.

Reading about great leaders and about the Teaching of discipleship does not make a good leader, but it helps us to improve the leadership of our personality. When leadership in the field of the personality is improved, the new leader emerges, graduated from the field of leadership of personality.

An experienced leader may closely see that his success in the field of service is based on those successes and victories which he carried on in the field of the personality. Our relationship with the world of our personality is reflected in the field in which we work. A leader can hardly be successful in life if he does not graduate from his relationship with his personality in his private life. If the foundation in his personal life is shaky, the leadership in the outer life will also be shaky.

Thinking is the process of giving form to energy. Through thinking energy materializes and a thoughtform is built.

The success of form building is thinking. Thoughtforms range from zero to Infinity — the deeper you think the better is your thoughtform, and the better is its influence or effect.

Through the thinking of people the energy of space turns into thoughtforms of mental matter and, it either pollutes the space or builds bridges in space for the ascent of humanity.

The leader first of all is a thinker. He builds bridges and ladders and highways for people to tread.

We had a teacher who built a school for private students. He was very careful with the construction work, especially with the passages, steps, and paths. One day he explained to us that he himself, with some assistance, built the school. After the work was completed he had a better idea of how to assist people to build their own characters. Every portion of the school corresponded to one of the portions of the student's character:

>foundation
>
>walls
>
>various rooms
>
>roof
>
>windows
>
>doors
>
>pathways

For him his school was a human being, a student, preparing for leadership work.

He told us that every student must be built like a building for a great purpose. Various equipment in it were parts of their character. Then one day he said, "We live in an organized building which is the replica of our nature. Every one of us lives as a school, in the school, as all of us within the school, live in the world-school."

He taught us to think. He said that all that you see in the world of matter is a result of human creativity, originated from thought.

Leadership understands that all is a school, and its duty is to build schools.

Sometimes spiritual people think that to build schools, man must inspire the will of their God on their students or followers. But this idea of God must be clear in the minds of leaders. The modern definition of God can be understood as One Who talks though our conscience, though our love, through our creativity, through compassion and goodness.

For some advancing human beings, the God idea is an idea of power, compassion and Light. God is

— you

— Father-Mother

— The power of the planet

— The power of the Sun

— The power of Cosmos

— The power of the Milky Way

— The power of that around which our Milky Way revolves

The idea of God is relative to your expanding consciousness. The more you expand your consciousness, the more inclusive is your God. There is One God, but Centers in the One God gradually can be approached.

Our bodies are the cells of the planet. Our souls are the cells in the Planetary Soul. It depends if you are conscious or not. Your soul can be part of the Solar Lord if awakened in a certain degree. It can be cells in the galactic Self. Every time your soul becomes a part of a greater soul, you take a major initiation. This is true for planetary, solar, and cosmic Souls.

If you are creating a school, start with natural science and let people see God in Nature. Then see God in most creative people. See God in every one, but do not define the undefinable. Let everyone approach God according to what he is.

Those who see God in Nature and God in man are those who will be able to see higher expressions of God in other dimensions. Creativity is the expressing of the idea of God at the level you are.

But, there is a sickness in spiritually oriented people, and at times it becomes epidemic. We call this sickness "spiritual fever." The signs of this sickness are as follows:

1. Over-devotional attitude

2. Strange behavior and over-attachment to the sanctuary, to the leader, and to the books

3. Overflowing givingness and offerings

4. Long hours of prayer, worship, and meditation

5. Indifference to daily duties and responsibilities

6. Exaggeration of humility and over-willingness to obey orders

7. Cherishing of transcendental views of dreams and visions

Let us take these individually.

1. Being over devotional is an attitude of a person who is always in the place of worship and always ready to force people that they must also be there to worship. His dressing and self-image change. He speaks softly, but criticizes, and shows that everything he does is for the glory of *his* God.

2. He attaches to the books, symbols, buildings, and the leader to show that he is burning with the fire of divine love. He endures criticism and people's negative emotions for the sake of his holy objects.

3. He overflows in givingness or offerings. He brings gifts to everyone who is in the same worship. He gives gifts especially to the leader. He wants to show everybody that he is infused with God. However when his fever passes he becomes the worst enemy to those whom he flooded with gifts and letters and flowers.

4. He sits for long hours in meditation or prayer suspended between earth and heaven. He is intoxicated with the mystery beyond his reasoning mind. This costs him later in the form of psychic disorders and physical diseases. Sometimes he burns his etheric and nervous fuses and he becomes an abnormal creature within his family and friends, causing them financial losses.

5. His spiritual fever makes him unresponsive toward his duties and responsibilities. He becomes careless toward his job and family duties. Sometimes this responsiveness bursts and turns into fanaticism and in that case he scorches everybody around him with his fire of "fever."

6. He develops exaggeration of humility and obedience to his superiors and obeys them to the letter. If he does not receive orders he fabricates them and obeys his own orders.

7. He overemphasizes his dreams, his viewpoints, his visions, and lives in them as if in a castle, and forgets about the existence of different viewpoints, his friends and his family members. Slowly he becomes a burden in society, and his behavior hurts the feelings of many.

After the spiritual fever passes such people become dry or cold, and then with all their might they plunge into the ocean of materialism and pleasures.

The most important point for the leader is that when people are in a "spiritual fever" he must be careful and not consider such people as being infused with the divine fire and psychic energy.

The real fire of the spirit gives reasoning, logic, temperance, solemnity to the subject, and he does not violate the freedom of people and their free choice. They become humble and avoid being show-offs, but increase in their labor, service, and striving. They become steady, persevering, progressing heights among human beings and therefore a help to many.

An understanding leader must refuse to accept gifts from those who are in spiritual fever. Neither must he promote them to higher duties and responsibilities, and wait until their fire has passed.

Be particularly cautious from those who bring big gifts to you and to your organization urged from a divine command. Actually be careful from those who, in their fever, bring big sums of money. Stop them and carefully reject them because they are acting under the obsession of fever.

Judas was an admirer of Jesus. Devadatta was an admirer of Buddha. They both came to earth in spiritual fever. Both betrayed their Masters.

Spirituality is not a fever. It is the light, the fire of steady preparation to serve and sacrifice, and to improve human relationships.

Leadership and the creating of an idea of God go together. Without creating there is no leadership. Without actualization of God there is no leadership, nor a God.

Leadership must be based on thinking, creative people, not followed with spiritual fever. The deeper the leader thinks, the clearer he sees his path. The deeper the leader thinks, the clearer he sees those "gods" who are born from vanity, ego, pride, hate, anger, and fear. These "gods" are obstacles on the path of humanity and the leadership must dissipate such thoughtforms if he wants to lead people into the true God of compassion, light, and beauty.

The power of the leader arises from his past experiences. If he had a position of leadership he naturally and instinctively chooses the right action in every thing, because in the past he failed many times. In his defeats he developed a store of experiences which act as an instinct. He naturally avoids those steps which would lead him to failure.

Thinking helps him to formulate his instincts to new conditions and make them fit these new conditions.

2
Leader and Love

All leaders must develop love along with true willpower and intellect. Willpower and intellect alone cannot do the job by themselves. The most important energy for a leader is the energy of love, fortified by willpower and intellect.

Love - compassion leads to synthesis and builds an identity on higher and higher planes.

Love builds identity. If you love someone, and if someone loves you, your identity is built. His or her love conceives your identity, which is further built by your love for him or her.

This identity can be on various planes. There is physical identity, emotional identity, mental identity, and the highest which is spiritual identity. This is the creativity of love, if it is real.

It is very important to create identity. Without identity, people have no self-respect. Self-respect evokes spiritual virtues to manifest. Lack of self-respect takes one into destructive paths.

The expression of real love nourishes the Chalice in the higher mind, and the magnetism of man increases in such a degree that it controls the operation of spatial energies that are necessary for health, happiness, success, prosperity, creativity, and contacts with Higher Worlds.

Creative energies that help and assist us are in space. They need to be called upon to participate in our creative plans. It is love that acts as the tune-in and key-in factors which then invoke the creative energies and draw them for help. Many people find their path ornamented with flowers and trees beyond their anticipation.

Selfishness and doubt do not live in real love. These two prime obstacles prevent the creative energies from helping us to prepare our future path.

Our identity grows as we see ourselves working with energies.

One day in my dream I saw an ocean with high waves. A voice told me that there is a wave among those waves which holds you always on top. I felt in my life that that wave was always there whenever I was engaged in a sacrificial loving job, duty, or responsibility.

As I see energies helping me, providing many friends and different assistants, my identity begins to grow with self-respect.

Identity and self-respect are not used for self-interest, but stand as a means for sacrificial service and self-renunciation. A man who has no identity is the victim of thousands of *selves* — pseudo I's, egos — emanating from glamors, illusions, and narcissism. That is why lack of identity is a punishment for oneself.

Real love is considered as an ocean which melts away all the powers of the ego. The ego is like pieces of ice in the field of your consciousness. If they are melted you feel oneness not only with yourself, but also with all life in general.

Love is a most magnetic substance. It is also a healing substance that accumulates within your aura. All creative energies make connection with the vortex of love in your aura, and they can make you a part of the cosmic creativity.

When someone loves you, he or she builds an image of you, an image so beautiful that he or she may love. That image continuously projected to you forms the nucleus of your identity. Love integrates you, and unconscious parts of yourself come together. Love psycho-synthesizes you.

When you love someone with deep love you pull yourself together to express that love. Physically, emotionally, and mentally you start to create a form, the nucleus of which is love.

The focusing process is the step taken for the creation of identity. You become "someone" to love "someone else."

This is the simplest way that this mystery of creating an identity can be explained. When we say that love creates identity we do not mean that it divides your beingness from the whole. Identity is an ever expanding concentric circle. You become a path of higher identities without losing your individuality.

To be an identity means to be an active center for Beauty, Goodness, Righteousness, Joy, Freedom, and creative energies for the service of all.

3
The Leader Faces Himself

The leader never humiliates or belittles himself with his own words or gestures. He expresses firmness, assurance, stability. He also respects those who demonstrate similar characteristics if they are based on a firm foundation.

When he faces something that he cannot do he does not say, "It is beyond my ability." But he says, "I am not ready to do it yet, or, I did not spend enough time to make myself ready to do it," and he encourages those who can do it.

A man can hypnotize himself and lose trust in himself when he humiliates or belittles himself in front of people. This is not an example to be an arrogant person who refuses to understand the limits of his abilities, but an example to respect his potentials, which can manifest in due time through his striving.

Also, a true leader does not impress himself with humiliating images that his enemies project to him through their belittling criticism and hatred. But he does not fail to see his defeats and failures. In such cases he does not fall into depression and apathy, or into self-condemnation, but tries to discover the causes and the ways through which he failed, and take serious steps not to yield to those causes.

Every failure of a leader is the beginning of a new ascension through a new discipline and striving to bring himself up-to-date.

A true leader works for Infinity, and if a failure lasts for days, weeks, even a lifetime he does not give up, because he knows that such moments of failure prepared him to hasten his speed of evolution in such a degree that the lost days and even lives will be gained back with interest.

The leader tries to see behind his life events the operation of the Law of Karma.

Many forces and energies released in the planet crisscross each other in the life of the leader manifesting as events. He observes them in a detached attitude, but in the meantime tries to see how the past causes can be handled in such a way that they do not tax his present life, but rather enrich his wisdom. Because of such an understanding, he does not judge and condemn others when they find themselves in similar situations.

Among his struggles with involutionary forces, the leader always fixes his heart to the ideal, and tries in every life to activate a part of that ideal.

Leadership Volume 2

©1996 The Creative Trust

All Rights Reserved: No part of this publication may be reproduced, stored in a retrieval system, or transmitted in any form, by any means, electronic, mechanical, photocopying, recording or otherwise, without permission in writing from the copyright owner or his representatives. Permission to quote is freely given. Contact publisher for details.

ISBN: 0-929874-51-X (Softcover)
ISBN: 0-929874-50-1 (Hardcover)

Library of Congress Catalog Card Number: 92-82864

Printed in the United States of America

Cover Design:	*Tim Fisher* Phoenix, Arizona
Printed by:	*Data Reproductions* Rochester Hills, Michigan
Published by:	**T.S.G. Publishing Foundation, Inc.** P.O. Box 7068 Cave Creek, AZ 85331-7068 United States of America

Note: Meditations and visualizations are given as guidelines. They should be used with discretion and after receiving professional advice.

2
Leader and Love

All leaders must develop love along with true willpower and intellect. Willpower and intellect alone cannot do the job by themselves. The most important energy for a leader is the energy of love, fortified by willpower and intellect.

Love - compassion leads to synthesis and builds an identity on higher and higher planes.

Love builds identity. If you love someone, and if someone loves you, your identity is built. His or her love conceives your identity, which is further built by your love for him or her.

This identity can be on various planes. There is physical identity, emotional identity, mental identity, and the highest which is spiritual identity. This is the creativity of love, if it is real.

It is very important to create identity. Without identity, people have no self-respect. Self-respect evokes spiritual virtues to manifest. Lack of self-respect takes one into destructive paths.

The expression of real love nourishes the Chalice in the higher mind, and the magnetism of man increases in such a degree that it controls the operation of spatial energies that are necessary for health, happiness, success, prosperity, creativity, and contacts with Higher Worlds.

Creative energies that help and assist us are in space. They need to be called upon to participate in our creative plans. It is love that acts as the tune-in and key-in factors which then invoke the creative energies and draw them for help. Many people find their path ornamented with flowers and trees beyond their anticipation.

Selfishness and doubt do not live in real love. These two prime obstacles prevent the creative energies from helping us to prepare our future path.

Our identity grows as we see ourselves working with energies.

One day in my dream I saw an ocean with high waves. A voice told me that there is a wave among those waves which holds you always on top. I felt in my life that that wave was always there whenever I was engaged in a sacrificial loving job, duty, or responsibility.

As I see energies helping me, providing many friends and different assistants, my identity begins to grow with self-respect.

Identity and self-respect are not used for self-interest, but stand as a means for sacrificial service and self-renunciation. A man who has no identity is the victim of thousands of *selves* — pseudo I's, egos — emanating from glamors, illusions, and narcissism. That is why lack of identity is a punishment for oneself.

Real love is considered as an ocean which melts away all the powers of the ego. The ego is like pieces of ice in the field of your consciousness. If they are melted you feel oneness not only with yourself, but also with all life in general.

Love is a most magnetic substance. It is also a healing substance that accumulates within your aura. All creative energies make connection with the vortex of love in your aura, and they can make you a part of the cosmic creativity.

When someone loves you, he or she builds an image of you, an image so beautiful that he or she may love. That image continuously projected to you forms the nucleus of your identity. Love integrates you, and unconscious parts of yourself come together. Love psycho-synthesizes you.

When you love someone with deep love you pull yourself together to express that love. Physically, emotionally, and mentally you start to create a form, the nucleus of which is love.

The focusing process is the step taken for the creation of identity. You become "someone" to love "someone else."

This is the simplest way that this mystery of creating an identity can be explained. When we say that love creates identity we do not mean that it divides your beingness from the whole. Identity is an ever expanding concentric circle. You become a path of higher identities without losing your individuality.

To be an identity means to be an active center for Beauty, Goodness, Righteousness, Joy, Freedom, and creative energies for the service of all.

3

The Leader Faces Himself

The leader never humiliates or belittles himself with his own words or gestures. He expresses firmness, assurance, stability. He also respects those who demonstrate similar characteristics if they are based on a firm foundation.

When he faces something that he cannot do he does not say, "It is beyond my ability." But he says, "I am not ready to do it yet, or, I did not spend enough time to make myself ready to do it," and he encourages those who can do it.

A man can hypnotize himself and lose trust in himself when he humiliates or belittles himself in front of people. This is not an example to be an arrogant person who refuses to understand the limits of his abilities, but an example to respect his potentials, which can manifest in due time through his striving.

Also, a true leader does not impress himself with humiliating images that his enemies project to him through their belittling criticism and hatred. But he does not fail to see his defeats and failures. In such cases he does not fall into depression and apathy, or into self-condemnation, but tries to discover the causes and the ways through which he failed, and take serious steps not to yield to those causes.

Every failure of a leader is the beginning of a new ascension through a new discipline and striving to bring himself up-to-date.

A true leader works for Infinity, and if a failure lasts for days, weeks, even a lifetime he does not give up, because he knows that such moments of failure prepared him to hasten his speed of evolution in such a degree that the lost days and even lives will be gained back with interest.

The leader tries to see behind his life events the operation of the Law of Karma.

Many forces and energies released in the planet crisscross each other in the life of the leader manifesting as events. He observes them in a detached attitude, but in the meantime tries to see how the past causes can be handled in such a way that they do not tax his present life, but rather enrich his wisdom. Because of such an understanding, he does not judge and condemn others when they find themselves in similar situations.

Among his struggles with involutionary forces, the leader always fixes his heart to the ideal, and tries in every life to activate a part of that ideal.

4

Personality and Leadership

There are so many beautiful people in the world with great talent and potentials, who have the urge to serve, to create, and to lead. But their personality is their greatest hindrance in the service and it makes their life half successful, sometimes even a total failure. Sometimes their life is a battlefield and their service greatly suffers.

Some people are control freaks; all they look for is to control, and thus they prevent their service from flowing spontaneously and freely in the fields of human need. They create reaction, refusal, rebellion, but their soul wants to clean the mess throughout their life.

Some of them are egotists. The egotists make their service useless, unattractive. People with good intentions refuse to cooperate with them and they leave them alone. Others get trapped in the force of the leader's ego, and build a group of egos, the most abhorrent circle of people, which eventually turns into a nest of self-seeking people.

Some people are handicapped with their vanity that they are everything, they can do everything, and they know everything. This prevents the flow of their soul energies for the service of others.

Vanity is a spiritually repulsive energy. It awakens the worse in human beings. If vain people join together they stop the progress of the people around themselves.

Some people are fond of arguments. They never do anything except after a lengthy argument. Argument creates a condition in which everyone forces his own will, and no cooperation is achieved.

Some people have various personality weaknesses. For example, sex is very much awakened in them and most of the time people around them are nothing else but sex objects. Such an attitude creates many problems and complications in their life and makes their leadership fail.

Other people, in spite of their deep spiritual feelings, have personality greed. They want to help themselves in every service. They look for reward, for personal benefit. Their love of matter blocks the giving rivers of their soul.

Some leaders' personality is full of jealousy. This burdens their soul. They prevent their soul's intention to promote people, to help them to achieve higher positions. They cannot stand it if somebody else shines. They are the ones that must be applauded, respected, and glorified. Jealousy, like an octopus, holds a person's spiritual hands and feet and renders him spiritually inactive. Thus many people have imprisoned souls, by the weakness of their personality.

Leaders must be extremely careful that their personality looks and behavior does not prevent the currents of their soul from pouring into the field of human need. They must observe themselves very closely to see if in any way their personality or personality interest is hindering their service.

Many beautiful souls not only are trapped in their personality weaknesses, but also the personality weaknesses of others — their husband, wife, relations, children — and because of them their service becomes very difficult.

Fanaticism is another personality hindrance. Fanaticism comes from crystallized thoughts which are inflamed through excited emotions. Fanatics prevent the flow of soul energy. A fanatical person cannot reach the souls of people but controls and affects the personalities, awakening in them violent emotions. Fanaticism prevents free communication and cooperation with the most essential. It restricts the free expression of soul energy.

There are lots of behavior patterns that work against the soul. For example, ugly or flashy dressing, too much makeup, ugly mannerisms, and inconsiderate behavior. All these prevent the service the soul is going to render.

Some people, in spite of having many talents, act as if they were nothing. Self-respect lacks in them, and they act as immature people in very serious conditions. This creates a wall between the soul and the field of service.

How Can We Open the Flow of Soul Energy?

The first step is to have faith in your talents and exercise and express them. Your virtues are parts of your talents. Without virtues the talent serves personality interests. These two must be cultivated together — talents and virtues. Virtues give talents the flow into the right direction.

Second, we need to observe any hindrance that we have in our personality and try to eradicate it.

Third, we need to start with creative meditation, visualizing the dramatization of our talents and virtues.

These three are the means which will surely open the channels of soul energy and eventually make the personality the tool of the soul.

Sometimes leaders think what a great service a person could do if he was not handicapped with such a vice, or such a mannerism, or such a selfishness, intolerance, anger, hate, jealousy, etc.

Sometimes people have such a bright soul, but are covered with a cloud of personality, karma, and pitfalls. A leader must help such people very carefully to open the flow of soul energies.

Some very talented people lose the opportunity to express their soul qualities because of their nosiness and aggressiveness. Whenever they work they try to be busy with things that are not their business. They are nosy with the lives of other personnel, with the personal affairs of their co-workers. They seek files and letters to satisfy their curiosity and sometimes fall into treason. They use all this information with an aggressive spirit which eventually "rewards" them with the needed information to give them power and control.

Many good workers lose the guidance of their Soul because of their nosiness and aggressiveness. These two qualities are in violation of privacy, and the interference in the business of others makes them personality oriented. Then the personality gets the higher end, and the Soul retreats and leaves the personality to suffer and to learn its lesson.

Many good workers are caught in this trap, evoking hatred and anger from their co-workers.

Not only has the spiritual man many talents, but also the personality may have many treasures which can be used in the work. For example, the personality can be rich, have properties and other possessions, can be healthy, strong, beautiful, can be rich in human communication, and can have many talents in business and human psychology. These can be used by the spiritual man when negativity, vices, and problems of the personality do not hinder the cooperation of the soul and personality.

When the soul can control and the personality responds to talents and the goals of the soul, then we have a person who is ready to serve humanity.

Soul and personality must be coordinated, integrated, and aligned so that the treasures of the soul are translated and used through a well prepared and disciplined personality.

5

Leadership Tests

A leader does not let unprepared ones stand in the whirlwinds. He observes, measures, tests the strength of his co-workers, and gradually leads them into the conditions where they are submitted to increasing pressure.

It is important to pass through physical pressures under increasing labor. It is important to pass through emotional pressures under excitement, fear, danger, upheavals. It is important to pass through mental pressures under problems, complicated conditions under strain and stress, under the demand of immediate needs or danger, or under heavy mental labor.

It is important to prepare a co-worker under the pressure of moral decisions, heroic actions, sacrifice, daring, and courage. If they pass through such tests, then the leader assigns duties to them to meet certain conditions and tests their strength.

A co-worker who had a high moral standard was sent on a mission with the most beautiful girls. He never came back and was lost with the girls without performing his responsibility.

A person was kept working beyond his eight hours. He left his job and went after his pleasures.

A real leader tests the strength of his co-workers before he exposes them to strong currents.

High performance cannot be obtained from co-workers unless they are tested again and again to their highest capacity.

A failed co-worker is the shame of the leader.

A leader must be cautious that his co-workers or those who are under training do not expose themselves to tasks for which they are unable to fulfill. Sometimes such failures can have drastic influence in their life.

The leader must give the duties that a co-worker can accomplish at least ninety percent. If he does it forty percent it is registered as a failure for the leadership.

As much as possible a worker must be tested physically, emotionally, mentally, and morally before he is assigned a specific job or duty. Specially when the co-worker is taking responsibility for many people, he must be trained more than an aircraft pilot, because he is not only responsible for their bodies, but for their spiritual future.

During the training the leader must discover various weaknesses and take steps to correct them again and again, until no trace remains from that weakness.

The co-worker under training must do the following:

— Be patient

— Not rebel

— See his improvement

— Expose himself entirely so that no trace of weakness is hidden

— Cultivate humility

— Ask power from his Self

— Respect the leader and surrender to his wisdom

— Be daring

— Never complain

It is better to be successful for three years than to live a life of failure in the field of labor for thirty years.

6
Leadership and Growth of Personality

The leader in all his relations with his co-workers must see that he cultivates their personality. This will be a great help to the work. He must be careful that he doesn't belittle them and hinder their personality growth. On the contrary, he must encourage their every effort to build up their personality.

For example, if his co-workers improve the way of their dressing and behavior he must acknowledge it. If they are able to improve their emotional responses or reactions he must encourage them. Every time they demonstrate the beauty of their emotions he must acknowledge it. If they improve their mental mechanism and thinking with various studies and disciplines he must encourage them and acknowledge them.

The true leader cannot cooperate with people around him who do not have their own personalities, with their own color and frequency. He does not want a uniform group around him with the same tonality, molded by the same patterns, but he needs personalities who demonstrate different qualities, powers, and originality so that his cooperation with them is multidimensional.

Without having a particular personality one cannot develop Soul-infusion and advance toward cooperation with the light within.

It is an utmost necessity to develop personalities in harmony with each other, personalities that complete each other and assist to evoke higher qualities from each other.

Personalities are built by cultivating the physical, emotional, and mental equipment by discipline, aspiration, meditation, and by striving. The personality vehicles — physical, emotional, and mental — must then integrate into one mechanism, and align with the light within.

Every personality must develop his or her ray qualities and try to harmonize himself with the ray qualities of others, thus achieve a most beautiful harmony with his co-workers.[1]

We must remember that behind every personality stands the true being. Each personality must try to express his true being through his actions and emotions and thoughts according to the character of his rays.

The true leader does not work with the souls of his co-workers if their personality is not taken care of and transformed and sublimated.

Every effort that his co-workers do to perfect their personalities evokes encouragement from a true leader. Appreciation of efforts leading to the cultivation of the personality is the duty of the leader.

Of course, the leader has the responsibility to make his co-workers understand that the development of the personality does not mean to lead themselves into ugliness, waste, and acquirement of nonessentials. Even if he sees that some of his co-workers are turning into crows and ornamenting themselves with the feathers of peacocks, he uses his wisdom to let them see it and come to their senses.

There are many spoiled children, but they carry in them the seeds of future glory.

Also, there is an important point which must be emphasized: the leader must see that his decisions, his orders, and commands must not be double-crossed by any co-worker working under him.

Often irresponsible co-workers change slightly or entirely a given decision, command, or rule from the leader or from the leadership, apparently believing that they are helping the leader. Every kind of misrepresentation must be stopped and those who are responsible for it must understand the seriousness of it.

The leader or leadership makes decisions and gives orders through co-measurement. Those who change the command can be shortsighted and create grave consequences.

Notes:

1. For detailed information on the rays, see the video, *The Seven Rays Interpreted*.

7

Employees and the Leader

In the old age a boss or a leader would scold an employee whenever the employee made a mistake or failed in his duties, and would then discharge the employee. In the future a boss will consult with the employee, discuss his problems, and either teach what the employee is lacking or send him to school for training.

An employee on the other hand must realize his mistake or failure and show a willingness to improve himself with openness, sincerity, and understanding. He must think how to improve the job so that both — the boss and employee — are benefited.

Consultation is a form of constructive criticism in which both the boss and the employee try to see the cause of failure, the form of failure, and take steps to annihilate the failure. The employee must try to benefit, if possible, by the experience of the boss.

The best and most lasting workers or employees are those who establish close communication with the boss in relation to their duties to see how they can better perform. In an important work or in critical times the employee must consult with the boss to have a new insight for his duties and secure new experience from his boss to use in his job.

The employee must not be prideful and think that he does not need advice. Discussions with the boss regarding certain performances or work deepen mutual trust, keep the boss up-to-date, and also develop closer cooperation with him.

It is very important for a worker or employee to try to discover the source of his mistakes or failures and not lament upon them with fear and anxiety. The important point is to try not to repeat his mistakes.

Sometimes the leader cannot see the mistakes of the worker. But a good worker notes and discusses them with the leader or boss. This adds confidence and trust, which are very necessary factors for success.

A good worker wants to be a good apparatus, complete in his parts, so that he renders a good service. A good leader wants the same thing. Building and tuning the apparatus do not hurt the employee nor the boss. Joy increases in their relationship if they can co-work without petty emotions and tensions. Daily consultations for a few moments take away the seeds of future tension.

Of course, an employee is not going to be a school boy or girl and ask if he can go to the bathroom. But if there is any doubt in him about a particular job, he must not hesitate to see his boss.

On the other hand, a leader or a boss may often let an employee make a wrong decision or even fail in his work in order to learn a lesson. He does not baby-sit him, but gives him enough freedom to decide and act, in the meantime keeping his eyes upon him.

A close communication with the boss is not to weaken his spirit of initiation and daring; on the contrary, it is to increase the spirit of initiation and daring. A wise leader helps an employee to move but lets him walk by himself.

In my father's pharmacy there was a head pharmacist who often consulted with my father. One day my father said that he was so well trained he could run the business without him. On another occasion he said, "I gave him so much vision that he has years to actualize it in his job." Another time he said, "Our minds are synchronized." He learned a lot from my father, but also my father developed in himself latent precious qualities.

Leaders are not those who create copies of themselves in others, but enrich others to cultivate their own talents.

You must not consult the leader in order to be closer to him and to secure his respect, or to secure your self-interest from others. Such a kind of relationship makes you empty of spirit. You must not expect respect from your leader because of your show-off or show of humility, nor should you expect respect from others because you are close to the leader.

Respect is a very complicated phenomenon. People try to be famous. Some work very hard to acquire fame. Some steal the fame of others. But the heart of the people sense the beingness in others, and if it is there, they respect those who have fame. Without solid respect there cannot be fame.

Once we saw a church in the wilderness which had long been abandoned. The bell was ringing due to the winds. Our Teacher said it was like a man who had fame but no respect.

You must evoke respect to secure the lasting of your fame. Fame is your achievement and good work, but respect is your inner attainment, inner culture, inner transformation.

Famous people are many but not all of them have the respect of the people. Those who run after fame will not evoke respect and they end their fame with shame.

How is respect formed? In respect there is *trust*. There is *admiration*. There is *recognition*. There is *approval*. If these feelings are not there, there is no real respect.

Many negative expectations can masquerade as respect as when you respect not the person but your self-interest. This is a horrible hypocrisy. To make people think you respect them — to secure your interests — is a self-defeating act.

8

Checking the Work

The leader periodically must check the work of his co-workers. He must see that they are working efficiently with the principles of cooperation and goal-fitness.

This checking process must not be a process of finding fault and condemnation or criticism. In no way must the leader belittle his co-workers. In the checking process the leader must not make the co-worker feel that the leader has no trust in him, but must make him feel that he is there to cooperate with him to make him more efficient, more organized, more fitting to the principle of work. Also the leader must make the co-worker feel that the leader is there to solve certain problems and prevent mistakes in the future.

The work must be checked at unexpected times at intervals of two to three months. If the co-worker is new, his work must be checked every two to three weeks.

The overall approach of the leader must be open. He must inspire trust and appreciation for the work done and encourage the worker to improve his work cultivating more efficiency.

The leader also must check:

1. The condition of the equipment his co-workers use, if

they are outdated and ready to be replaced.

2. If the desk, table, and room are in ideal condition for the work.

3. If the worker has any complaints about his health or his communication with others.

Thus the leader must be interested about all the conditions in which the co-worker carries out his duties and improve the conditions if it is possible.

The leader can also clean any misunderstanding existing between the co-worker and himself. The best work is done in harmony and understanding. The leader must inspire his co-workers and show them that he trusts them and he is ready to assist them to be more efficient.

The leader must cultivate the consciousness of his co-workers so that each one's efficiency contributes to the success of the entire work. That one bolt that is not properly working in the engine can be responsible for the failure of the whole engine.

The leader must not give the impression that his co-workers are his slaves, but make them realize that he is a servant of each of them to make them more efficient.

Co-workers, apart from having a strong self-trust of their work, must consider that exposing themselves to the eyes of the leader will tremendously increase their efficiency and cooperation.

Co-workers are not those who hide in the halls of their mistakes and guard that hall by all means. On the contrary, they want the light of the leader to penetrate into their every action, so that no non-goalfitting action spreads roots in their work. True group consciousness brings everything into the light.

The leader must communicate with his co-workers not only in checking their work, but also in making them realize that he is ready for any help that they need.

9

Leader to Be

A leader is a diamond with a thousand facets.

A leader avoids encouraging those people who have egos, but at the same time urges them to study, meditate, and serve. To help them the leader, for a long time, shows indifference toward them by not giving a chance to

> 1. lecture
>
> 2. occupy positions
>
> 3. be active in committees

He analyzes their reactions to his indifference. Through the filter of his indifference he filters gradually their vanity, ego, self-interests, and waits until he sees that they show humility and indifference to praise and positions, and adhere to spiritual development and cooperation.

The leader is very cautious with aggressive, self-asserting people because they act from the center of ego and vanity, and they ruin the job given to them. Every job done by vain and aggressive people cultivates similar vices in their co-workers.

On many occasions to test his co-workers, the leader must stand in the shadow and let his co-workers do the job and watch their behavior. If they are shielded by indifference to public response, then he may promote them to higher tasks, knowing they are shielded by their sincerity.

A leader must be very careful not to inflame the ego in his co-workers, but try to eliminate it.

A true co-worker is interested in the work to be done, not interested about who does the work. Whoever does the work, he feels as if he did it. He does not impose himself or the leader to do the job. The leader is very careful not to encourage in his co-workers any sign of show-off. Those who can pass the filter of indifference can be expected to be great leaders in the future.

Understand that under indifference of a leader there is keen observation for the one toward which he is indifferent.

In his indifference he builds the character of his co-workers which he hopes will endure until traces of show-off vanish.

The signs of true leaders to be are:

1. They like to renounce their desire to be praised or recognized

2. In any labor they appreciate the work done by others

3. They are indifferent toward any praise, success, and defeat

4. They do not blame anyone for their failure, and they do not praise themselves for any success

5. They strive for self-abnegation

6. They let the most essential assist their actions and labor

7. They never look for position

Through a real leader the Plan works, the Masters and the Hierarchy work. He is aware that his leadership is inspired from true higher sources, and he does not care if people recognize him or not.

The leader sincerely and deeply loves those toward whom he is "indifferent" — and his love sustains them through their tense period, while his co-workers deepen the roots of their true spirituality.

He promotes them very slowly, until he is sure that dangerous elements in them have no chance to ruin them and their labor.

The leader looks upon his co-workers not for a week, month, years, but for a lifetime. One life is worthy of preparing oneself for ten lives of future leadership. The iron must be tempered for the heavy labor of the future.

Leadership is not for short-sighted people with a short-ranged sense of time. Leadership is for those who do not count months, years, and a lifetime as long as the diamond in them is building.

One day a student said to the Teacher, "Christ wasted thirty years to serve three years." He answered, "Christ prepared Himself ten years for each year's labor. Who knows how many hundreds of years he disciplined Himself to be able to have ten years' preparation for one year's labor.

A leader's labor is just like a wild horse. A wild horse is the field of his labor and personality. He must tame it every minute, because this wild horse shows unexpected movements in unexpected moments. But the leader continues to ride that horse even if he is thrown from his back many times. He mounts again on the back of the horse until he tames him and controls him as best as possible.

Real leaders are praised by their wounds, and today's wound becomes their future glory.

Leadership is continuity, persevering in the mastery of the personality and the field of service in "self-forgetfulness, harmlessness, and right speech."

10

Experience

When people see, hear, taste, smell, and touch any object in any form or intensity they call it experience. These events, happenings, tragedies, or pleasant moments are experiences to them.

Also they call inner events, contacts, joy, sorrow, visualization, imagination, and creativity experiences. Any event recognized by our mind becomes experience.

It is important to notice that a real experience is a real wisdom, a real knowledge that is recorded by most of your senses. The awareness of what happened is not a true experience. Experience is the knowledge of why it happened, and what can be its consequences, recorded by "our" mind.[1]

To gain certain experiences you must pay heavily, and also you must be prepared to benefit from the experiences.

There are negative experiences and positive experiences. There are lesser experiences and greater experiences. Negative experiences are those which limit your freedom, your joy, your expansion, and cause pain and suffering.

If you do not know the cause of these experiences, and if you have no control over them, and do not have an inner mechanism to transform them, they are not counted as experiences — mostly because you cannot avoid them. You cannot stop them from repeating.

Positive experiences are those which expand the fields of your activities, increase your joy, your health, prosperity, give you more freedom and greater striving.

Lesser experiences are related to your lower centers or lower bodies. Greater experiences are related to your higher senses, higher bodies, higher planes. Also, greater experiences are related to spiritual contacts and spiritual creativity.

In greater experiences your heart center, throat center, ajna center, head center, and the Chalice are involved with their higher correspondences on higher planes. Also, the higher experiences are related to group life, national life, global life, even solar life.

In lesser experiences your sacral center, solar plexus and base of spine are involved, and all your lesser experiences are related to your individual life, personality, self-interest, and family interest.

There is also a kind of experience which is imposed upon us. Unexpected attacks, help, supermundane intervention, obsession, possession, *tulku*, all are imposed experiences. It is some force outside of you that takes control over you and functions through you. This experience can be voluntary or involuntary. In both cases you can experience in various degrees and with various reactions and responses. If you are aware of the plane of forces controlling you and you cooperate you may harvest a lot of experiences.

All life proceeds toward higher levels only by the means of experience. Neither your knowledge nor your diplomas can help you to move forward toward a spiritual height. It is only your experiences that pave the way toward your soul's destination.

The effect of your experiences can be enormous upon the racial consciousness and on the speed of people's evolution.

It is the energy emanating from your experiences that moves the cultures and civilizations ahead.

Experience must control the application of your knowledge. If not, your knowledge turns into an instrument of destruction. Similarly your experience must guide your relationships with other people, or else your relationships present a source of trouble for you.

If your glamors, illusions, knowledge, blind urges and drives are controlling you instead of your experience, you soon become a slave not only to the forces of your personality but also to the hands of dark forces.

Every time you plan something, listen to the voice of your experiences and follow that voice to the end.

Most people call their habits, fears, and hypnotic suggestions experiences. Because by the force of their habits, fears, and posthypnotic suggestions they can control certain events, stop them or start them.

Experiences are the accumulated wisdom of years and lives. Experiences make new ways and energies available for you to make breakthroughs and to walk on the highway of virtues — harmlessness, fearlessness, and renunciation. Experience always chooses Beauty, Goodness, and Righteousness. These are the signs of true experiences.

Once a person said, "I have had bad experiences. Every time I started a business and became successful I destroyed my businesses because of fear which paralyzed me during the time of the most important decisions. Now that this is my experience, I will never dare again to start a new business."

This person was not acting through an experience, but through a cause that was hidden behind his failure. He never thoroughly searched for the true cause of his failure, and his "experience" of failure or the event of failure became for him a stop sign or a red light on his road.

It is true that the memories of past failures, which people like to call experiences, prevent us from achieving success. But we must create subjective experiences to break the walls of such past memories. One of the means to do that is intense visualization of yourself being highly successful, in any field you want, and dramatize that success in detail for a long time. The result will be that such a visualization slowly becomes your experience. The wall of past memories will fall down, and you will make your breakthrough.

Thus, consciously building up experiences through your visualization you conquer the thoughtform that hinders you.

Real experience is always the start for success on the path of perfection.

Visualization can provide the opportunity so that our experiences on the mental plane can slowly descend to the astral and etheric planes, and the forces of life can bring into actualization on the physical plane those experiences which you had in the mental plane.

This is how higher creativity is contacted to pave the way for the success of the spirit.

A higher moment of creativity is when you are engaged in the labor of contacting higher ideas, visions, and revelations, and bringing them to formulation, dramatization, and expression.

Creativity is an immense labor and the process of it offers some very rare experiences when you deal with the highest you contain, and with the highest that you contact.

Such experiences are very rare when you transform your nature and enable your self to be an instrument of transmitting the energy of higher contacts into formulations which will accelerate the transformation process on earth.

There are also experiences of horror and death, which stimulate various centers within our system, and evoke different faces of reality existing within us.

Some Great Ones pass through experiences of extreme loneliness, moments of total vacuum, or total unity with all that exists.

All these experiences are the result of our karma, and also tests and crises on our path to lead us toward greater maturity.

There are other experiences which are gained by those who consciously withdraw from the physical, astral, and mental planes and enter the Intuitional Plane. Can you imagine what an amount of knowledge is collected on this path of conscious withdrawal from the bodies, their worlds, and by conscious observation of what occurs during such a journey?

When such a person comes back he is a wealthy man in spirit, full of knowledge and wisdom according to his soul Ray. This is how the world consciousness is enriched and expanded. Every conscious breakthrough to Higher Worlds brings to the world a more abundant life.

The experiences of the past become the instinct of the present. We do things as if we know about them and how to do them.

When people advance they can surpass their period of being through experimentation by using their logic and reasoning. Logic and reasoning lead to a knowledge which is superior to experience in its use.

Experiences of the past do not always fit the conditions of the present. Life always progresses and experiences of the past cannot be reliable without reasoning and logic.

Experience is an apparatus which must be kept up-to-date by additional experience or by logic.

There is a difference between logic and reasoning. Logic follows an inner subjective standard. Reasoning is a strong labor to find things as they are, or as they affect the environment.

In logic you try to see things from inside to the outside. In reasoning you try to see from the outside to the inside.

Experience is the way of the universal consciousness to teach you through the events going on in life.

Experience is a treasure house from which you can use anything that fits the present situation with some additions and subtractions. Some people forcefully advise people to follow their own experience. This does not always help those who are advised because of the changing conditions of life.

Logic is more up-to-date than experience. When logic, reasoning, and experience are combined you have a powerful individuality who can lead people.

Logic is subjectively controlled by the standard of the soul. The soul is the logic of man, and logic is the exercise of the soul to communicate with the outer man. It operates through inner standards which are there as guidance.

Not everybody has access to logic. Reasoning is an effort to develop logic. Logic turns into a discriminating faculty and then it proceeds toward intuition.

The intuition acts as a superior instinct, or as the essence of experience, reasoning, and logic. These three are synthesized in the intuition.

Reasoning is lower mental.

Logic is higher mental functioning with the lower mind.

Instinct is etheric.

Experience can be etheric, astral, mental, which can be synthesized in the etheric centers.

Notes:

1. See also *Ageless Wisdom*, Ch. 24 "Experience".

11

Guidelines for Organizing a Correspondence Course

Three main requirements on the path of spiritual unfoldment are

1. Certainty

2. Balance

3. Concentration

These three contribute to your mental health. Without them you cannot proceed on the Path and you cannot serve humanity.

What should a student do to gain or maintain certainty, balance, and concentration?

In correspondence courses it must be strongly emphasized that meditation and other mental and "spiritual" practices are very dangerous if not handled in the right way.[1]

Correspondence courses are an important part of leadership and group work. It is the training ground for future leaders.

Correspondence courses should suggest that the student not follow different practices at the same time. He should follow one teacher, or one line of spiritual discipline. Mixing teachers and spiritual practices creates confusion. Actually, every change of spiritual practice must only be followed after the advice of the former teacher and with the consultation of the new teacher.

The student is a precious soul. He should not submit himself to those who claim they are psychics, teachers, initiates, or masters. By their fruits you will know them and by the light of your Intuition you must be guided.

New instructions should not be sent to those who are unable to discriminate in their readings, in their spiritual practices, or in choosing their teachers. Instructions or study sets should no longer be sent to those who engage in various practices to develop psychic powers, to open their chakras, or to gain control over others. Lessons sets should no longer be sent if the secretarial committee which oversees the courses is informed that:

1. The student uses drugs

2. The student is engaged in crimes

3. The student lives an unwholesome sexual life

One can advance on the spiritual path through right meditation and by living a virtuous life, in simplicity and honesty.

Certainty can be achieved if you do not fall into confusion. Confusion is mental indigestion. Confusion is caused when you "eat" things you cannot digest, or when you follow practices which create disturbances in your psychic mechanism.

Balance is achieved when you live a virtuous life and do not disturb your mind with various contradictory teachings and exercises.

Concentration is achieved when you try to live according to your highest vision or ideal.

The secretarial committee must deal very carefully with those students who are in a hurry, who are lazy, or who are subject to various psychic influences. The main objective of the course should be to foster mental health in the student and to develop a mind that can think independently, clearly, and in the light of the Soul.

A student must reach a certain stage of maturity before he exercises pure discrimination. That is why we have Teachers. The most important role of the Teacher is to help you develop discrimination. To reach that destination the Teacher tries to help you learn *thinking*. He wants you to stand on your feet and depend upon the resources found within your Self. He wants you to protect yourself from those whose interest is not for your progress.

The Teacher wants you to learn to run your own life in the light of your Soul. The teacher does not want you to believe the words of psychics, aura readers, past life readers but instead to try to find the truth within yourself.

It must be stressed that the course is not for those who follow the path of hypnotism, mediums, and those who contact the dead. The course will have nothing in common with these people.

Certainty comes if you learn and apply the virtues. Balance comes if you live under the light of your conscience. Concentration comes if you do not scatter yourself.

After presenting these ideas to the prospective correspondence course student, he may be offered the course if he chooses. The secretarial group must emphasize at this time that the student can drop his study with the course any time he wants. But if he chooses to follow the course, he must follow it exactly as it is given to him, of his own free will, and at his own risk.

The correspondence course will consist of a series of study sets which include: material from the Teaching to be studied, meditation seed thoughts for the study period, work to be done composed of exercises and recording of seed thoughts. At the end of the study period, the student will send in a paper on the subject assigned and a report on his daily meditation. The lessons are designed to last one month, although the pace of individual students may vary.

The student's paper is answered by a secretary or a secretarial group. If an individual secretary answer the papers, the secretary's letter should be checked by the secretarial committee.

Students are assigned a number which they use on their papers. Anonymity, whenever possible, helps to avoid the influence of personal feelings and prejudice in the work.

The secretarial group is formed as a training ground for the secretaries. The goal of the secretarial group is to learn how to be working tools to solve their own problems and the problems of others.

In order to improve his knowledge, his sensitivity, and his technique, the secretary must show a live interest in the papers of the student as well as the student's life and psychology, *without any personality reaction*. The student's paper is an expression of his life, and it often reflects his physical, emotional, mental, and spiritual conditions.

The main focus of the secretary will be on the paper of the student, not on the student personally. The secretary will have no active interest in the student's personality life except when he is forced to emphasize certain principles. For example, the secretary does not need to say, "Your smoking is not good for your brain." Instead he can say, "Smoking is not considered beneficial for those who are engaged in meditation."

In his letter the secretary will always try to create focus. The secretary must try to concentrate the student's attention and interest on the subject itself. After focusing his consciousness on the lesson, the secretary's explanation should be a beginning, not an end. This is the secret of making the student try to go deeper than the secretary did in his letter.

In this way the secretary fosters in the student the spirit of *search* or *research*. The secretary must not present the whole idea to the students but instead must let him labor to find out more and feel the joy of finding more.

The secretary must bring to the student's attention the seed thought of his meditation. Meditation on the seed thought presented to the student will create a group energy field which can be used for various services.

No instruction is valid unless it is digested and assimilated through meditation. The major intention of the course will not be to give information but to train students in meditation so that they themselves may find out the information they need for their future.

The main purpose of the secretary's letters is to make the student deeply interested and occupied in meditation.

The meditation report must be carefully analyzed and compared with the past report so that the secretary can see if the student is progressing in his thinking. If necessary, the secretary may make some remarks about the deeper layers of the seed thought in order to create an interest in the student to go deeper in his own meditation.

The secretary must be thoroughly familiar with whatever the student is studying. When the secretary studies the lessons as well, it paves the way for the student to understand the lessons better. Through his letters the secretary creates a rapport with the student, and on certain occasions his knowledge flows into the student's mind and makes him more able to grasp his lessons.

The secretary has a very important responsibility to his student. If he does not really love his job, he will channel negativity to the student and eventually make him drop the course. Any secretary who does not have wholehearted dedication and love for his work should resign.

The secretary must always give *encouragement*. He must not use criticism. The negative points in a student's paper — points which are out of order, ugly, wrongly motivated, or self-assertive — must be totally ignored by the secretary in his letter. Instead the secretary must very indirectly and subtly lead the student to higher ideas and attitudes.

This will happen naturally if the secretary inspires the student to study his lessons and do regular daily meditation.

When the secretary turns the student's attention to the negative points in his paper, the secretary may create many undesirable reactions in the student:

1. The student may go deeper into his negativity to protect his feelings and save his face.

2. He may attack the secretary.

3. He may leave the Teaching.

The secretary must beautifully and indirectly emphasize positive counterparts to the student's negative ideas. He must direct the student's attention to the future. At the end of his letter the secretary must suggest a vision toward which the student is striving.

The most successful letter is the one that converses with the student. The student must feel that there is someone at the other end of the line who has an active interest in him.

All information about the student is strictly confidential, including his name and address. Even if the student wants information released to others, the secretary will not do it. Secretaries will not share the student's letters or information with anyone, not even their husbands or wives.

There must be an occult confidence between the secretary and the student, and this confidence must be sustained forever by all means.

Secretaries may discuss problems and various questions related to their students at conferences of secretaries, but these questions must be raised with no mention nor even a subtle inference about the source. If a problem is being discussed at a conference about a particular student and his identity is easily recognizable, the secretary will be very careful that he does not reveal any information about the student through his smiles, gestures, jokes, or other expressions.

The secretarial group must exercise strict discipline to maintain the confidentiality of personal information in order to avoid complicated problems.

If a secretary ever wishes to consult a psychologist or psychiatrist in answering a student, he must go through the group leader in order to avoid any problems. The leader will find the best way to assist the secretary and the student in handling such a situation.

A secretary is not a teacher. The Teaching is given to the student in his study sets. The duty of the secretary is to encourage the student and focus his attention on some points he did not see through a few suggestions.

The secretary must stand by his student as a source of energy, courage, and inspiration. The secretary is an *inspirer*.

When a student asks a question, the secretary must direct him to a book or chapter or a specific place in his study sets. He may also tell the student that his questions will be answered as his studies deepen and his meditation becomes more regular. The secretary may also answer the student's questions by posing new questions to him.

The secretary is never obliged to answer any questions of his student which make him feel uncomfortable.

Some students ask questions before they are ready for the answers. In such cases the secretary must postpone answering the questions or prepare the student for future realizations. But if a question demonstrates vanity, unreadiness, or a spirit of ridiculing the Teacher, the student may totally neglect the question or give a sharp lesson.

The secretary must be tolerant of the motives by which a student is drawn to the Teaching. His motive or his racial, national, political, or religious background must never create prejudices in the secretary.

The secretary must deal with the Soul of his student. The secretary must direct his words to the student's Soul. He must always beware of giving advice; he must instead tell the student to deal with his problem through his Soul or through specialists. Personality help must eventually come from one's own Soul.

A student may belong to any religion or group. The secretary may have negative or positive feelings about the religion or group the student is attached to, but he will try to stand above his feelings and focus his mind on the Teaching.

If a student persistently wants to advertise his religious beliefs, for example, the secretary may bring to his attention that the course has no religious discrimination and all Great Ones came from the same Source of Light.

The secretary must not write about his political views and choice of candidates or issues, even if the student asks his opinion.

The secretary's letter must be short, not more than one half to one page long. The letter must be condensed and focused. In learning how to write a short letter, the secretary learns to use his mind in a synthesizing way. He must make his letter like a seed thought in his student's mind, instead of meditating for the student in his letter.

It is very important that the secretary give ample time to the study of the student's papers so that he can answer the student to the best of his ability.

The secretary's letter must always carry joy and enthusiasm.

The secretary must not condemn, criticize, or praise his student. Praise and criticism focus the mind of the student on his personality. Encouragement is not praise. Analysis is not criticism.

Here are some technical points to consider:

1. Students' papers come to the central office where they are delegated to individual secretaries.

2. Secretaries return their answers to the central office. After approval, the answer is mailed to the student from the central office.

3. Secretaries should submit a copy of their answer, signed personally. The copy stays on file in the central office.

4. The secretary's letter should begin "Dear Fellow Student (first name)." The letter should be signed "The Meditation Correspondence Course Secretarial Committee."

5. The envelope should be addressed in the central office.

6. Secretaries will be reassigned periodically to prevent building any close personal relationship between secretary and student.

In secretarial relationships any personality attachment must be rejected immediately. If a secretary cannot operate above the personality level, he presents a danger for the group either by lowering the standards of the leadership group or by creating complicating communications.

The secretarial group must meet periodically, at least once every two months if possible, to discuss any questions, problems, or needs.

All student papers must be answered promptly, within one week whenever possible. Delayed letters lose their intensity and meaning.

Above all, the secretary must always remember that the student is a gift sent to him by karma; he is a precious soul.

Each student who comes to you is a gift for you:

1. Students develop a greater sense of responsibility in you.

2. Students make you learn how to lead.

3. Students expand your consciousness by urging you to find better responses.

Another very important point for your attention is that some secretaries give too much praise. What does this do?

1. It makes the student feel that he is more than what he

really is.

2. It slows down his striving.

3. The student loses interest in the Teaching.

4. He develops ego.

5. He loses faith in the secretary.

The golden mean between criticism and balance must be found.

What can you actually do?

1. Emphasize the ideas that are really good, but not as though the ideas belong to the student.

Sometimes people do not realize what they are writing. Sometimes they copy others; sometimes it is subconscious; sometimes it is telepathic. Considering all these cases, you must draw their attention to the exceptional ideas you find in their writing and make them look at them more carefully, with deeper understanding.

You must know that not everyone is consciously aware of what he writes.

2. By giving them a chance to read their ideas or thoughts once more, you very gracefully reveal to them the depths of certain ideas that perhaps they never realized. Or you can point out certain effects that their ideas can have.

You must know that often their ideas are not related to the past, present, or future and the effects are not considered. Most of their ideas are decorations brought out in their writing to show-off.

Most of you have done or are doing the same thing, so you must be familiar with this point.

3. After using points #1 and #2, then refer to an idea which is related to the student's ideas but reveals a deeper side of them.

Remember, we must not develop ego and vanity in our students but clarity and striving.

Notes:

1. See *The Psyche and Psychism*, Chs. 32, 40, 71.

12

The Formulations of Law

There are many *Laws*. Laws are impositions of Will. A man, a group, a government, a planetary Life, a solar Life, a galactic Life, the Cosmic Life — all these lives have their own will. When they formulate their will, we have laws.

Laws are formulated according to the need of the time or cycle. Laws are not permanent; they work, they create confusion, they become obsolete, and they pass away in time and space.

Laws are formulated according to the need of the object or subject, according to the demand of the time, according to the levels of the object or subject, according to the relationship of the object to higher and lower lives. When the need, the cycle, the level, or the relationship changes, the former laws do not work any more and new laws are formulated.

If the source of the law is more advanced and more universal, the laws he creates last longer and create better results.

Laws are created for any of the following reasons:

1. To exploit people

2. To unite people

3. To create right human relations

4. To create order and protection

5. To inspire striving and progress

6. To create group consciousness — sharing

7. To inspire transformation

8. To inspire revelation

9. To inspire synthesis

Laws are reinforced by power or by Intuition. Power is given to a man or a group by an act of violence by the man or the group, by the weakness and ignorance of the subjects, or by the intuitive understanding of the subjects.

Power lasts if the man or the group in power is interested in its own welfare and has enough ways and means to impose itself upon its subjects. Power diminishes when the subjects see the uselessness of the former laws, organize, and create different laws to impose on the leadership. Power also diminishes when the group or man in power no longer sees the need for power and hands the power to one who is far more advanced.

All these changes of power progress either through revolutions, wars, social disturbances, blood and pain, or through understanding and acceptance.

Laws are divided into four categories:

1. There are laws formulated for the physical, emotional, and mental interests of individuals or groups.

2. There are laws formulated to translate the Will of One in Whom we live, move, and have our being.

3. There are laws formulated to adapt human interests to the Divine interest.

4. There are laws formulated to execute principles.

The best way to make laws understood and followed is to educate people and make them realize that laws are formulated to bring them health, happiness, and prosperity and to create conditions for their moral and spiritual development.

On the other hand, the executors of laws must live a life that is an example for others. They must not use the laws to suppress people or try to use people as their own property.

If such considerations are not followed the laws can be used as tools to impose self or group interest upon the people. It is through such an imposition of law that totalitarianism comes into being, and the laws that were created to secure the freedom and progress of people turn into laws that breed slavery, fear, dependency, and confusion.

Laws must be formulated to execute universal principles and educate people to secure their cooperation.

For example, the principle of essential divinity is the source of major laws, but people do not realize the source. If a law does not execute the principle from which it originated, it turns against itself and paves the way for totalitarianism.

We can divide laws in the following way:

1. Laws that pursue self- or separative interest.

2. Laws that promise freedom and prosperity.

3. Laws that promise victory over oneself.

4. Laws that formulate and execute *principles*.

The first group of laws end in anarchy.

Totalitarianism always defeats itself because it is the tool of those people whose interests are their separative selves, their pleasures, or their hatreds, fears, and greed. When the foundation is separatism, pleasure of body, hatred, fear, and greed, no building will last long and the depth of its destruction will be equal to its height.

The second and the fourth group of laws were formulated by great Ones such as Krishna, Buddha, Zoroaster, Christ, Hercules, Moses, Mohammed, and Their disciples. These Great Ones demonstrated the laws through Their lives. Their lives were the formulations of the laws.

Their laws, which were an effort to translate the Will and Purpose of the One in Whom we live, move, and have our being, were generally opposed by the first group of laws. Or, Their laws slowly degenerated in the minds of those who grasped them but did not make efforts to live them. Such laws can only by understood by living the laws and making the laws part of one's being. In other words, these great laws cannot be understood and carried out if the person does not raise his level of beingness through the transformation of his life to the level where the laws are given. Such laws can be grasped and assimilated only where the laws were given — "on the top of the mountain," not "in the valley."

The third kind of laws resulted from the labor of those who tried to understand these higher laws and adapt them to the life of the masses. Through such an effort, philosophies, religions, and churches came into being. But because the group of Great Ones Who formulated the Will of the Great Life and the group who tried to adapt their formulated laws to the life in general did not believe in forced power, they were slowly overruled by the totalitarian will of the first group. This happened age after age, in one form or another under various guises and names.

Watch the film of history and your eyes will see it clearly.

Totalitarian law became the darkest obstacle for the progress of humanity. Totalitarianism is a widespread system working through many ways, means, and forms in the politics of all nations, in the education of all nations, and in the philosophy of all nations. You can see its success in the arts, psychology, communication, and the media. You can see its immense success in science and the application of science. Once science and the scientific mind fall under the force of totalitarianism, it is the signal that the destruction of our culture and civilization is at hand.

Totalitarianism has also penetrated into religious institutions. A grave danger for the future lies there. Totalitarianism is now infiltrating and invading the whole economic system of the world, slowly taking under its control money, energy (gas, water, electricity, food), clothing, and housing. Through what a disaster humanity will pass if totalitarianism controls the economy of the nations.

The defeat of totalitarianism is only carried out through right education and by raising the level of consciousness of the masses. But totalitarianism knows this, and it has made all efforts to take the educational institutions into its own hands all over the world, in every country.

A great Sage once said that the greatest enemy of humanity is totalitarianism. It is clear that most contemporary laws are created by totalitarians or by those people who are unconsciously serving totalitarianism.

To make itself survive, totalitarianism created a vicious circle of world problems and a situation in which one cannot pull a nail from the wall without destroying the wall. People are now inclined to think that only a *total destruction* may clear the mess which human ignorance, in collaboration with dark forces, created in the world.

Will total destruction be the victory of the forces of freedom, light, and love? Will not human beings go through the same pattern and create another Atlantis?

Where is the road to salvation? How will it be possible to guide this humanity safely to its Divine destination?

13

Leadership and the Law of Repulsion

The Law of Repulsion is one of the laws of group work.

This law concerns itself with the ability of an atom to throw off, or refuse to contact, any energy deemed inimical to group activity. It is literally a law of service, but only comes consciously into play when the atom has established certain basic discriminations, and guides its activities through the knowledge of the laws of its own being. This law is not the same as the Law of Repulsion which is used in connection with the Law of Attraction between forms which have relation to the material. The laws we are now considering have relation to the psyche, or to the Vishnu aspect. One group of laws concern energies emanating from the physical sun; the ones we are now considering emanate from the heart of the Sun. The "repulsion" here dealt with has the effect (when consciously applied through the developed heart energy of a human atom, for instance) of furthering the interests of the repulsed unit and of driving this unit closer to its own centre. Perhaps some idea of the great beauty of this law as it works out can be gathered from an occult phrase in a certain old book:

"This repulsive force drives in seven directions, and forces all that it contacts back to the bosom of the seven spiritual fathers."[1]

The Law of Repulsion is a very interesting law which works in group life and in the life of Hierarchies. The Heart of the Sun provides this energy, which works as a law. In the heart of each human being and in the heart of each group this energy exists. It must be brought into activity. The heart must repulse all who are now ready to stand on their own feet and carry on their own salvation with their own hands and feet. If this law is not active in the heart of the group leader, slavery, totalitarianism, and exploitation are the results.

The eagle must repulse his children to leave the nest and fly. The Law of Repulsion is based on compassion, insight, foresight, and Divine indifference.

The leader and the group members must not be sticky with each other. They must allow each other to be what they want to be. And when the time comes that the leader feels it is better for a member to stand away to develop his own power and integrity, he will *repulse* him — esoterically. A member can hurt the growth of the group if he is advancing too fast, or accumulating too much power.

The repulsed member can also hurt himself and the group if the group limits his expansion and freedom. In both cases the leader or the heart of the group must repulse him.

This also happens when a person comes with good intentions, but his ray formation does not bring beneficial results in the group. The leader repulses him to go and find the right place for his right growth.

Those who have the First Ray predominating in their nature can naturally do such a job. They have no attachments, and because of this they see the issue clearly and act indifferently.

Of course, sometimes the leader receives violent reactions from those whom he repulses, but this is considered his sacrificial responsibility. No matter how they react, whether they love or hate, appreciate or condemn, he repulses them only to render a service to the souls of those whom he repulses.

The Law of Repulsion also operates within the group members. Certain members repulse others. But the repulsion does not create cleavages or problems. The group member knows that keeping a good distance from a certain member is very beneficial for his own Path and also for the Path of the other person. He consciously repulses certain members for various reasons, but all of these repulsions are based upon compassion and on the desire to keep the Path of the group free of obstacles, problems, and complications and to serve the Plan.

To repulse a member or a fellow member requires an aura which is not sticky. There are auras which are sticky and auras which resemble electrical spheres. Sticky auras are built of large amounts of uncontrolled desires, drives, and urges. They try to satisfy themselves through any opportunity, and thus establish personal links and fusions. It is such members who create problems when their saturation points are reached and rejection begins.

Rejection is not repulsion. In rejection there is fear, hatred, anger, greed, and jealousy. In repulsion there is control, indifference, pure love for the future, and deep understanding.

This is literally "the law of service" by which man repulses nonessentials and works only for the most essential. He sacrifices all that will hinder the progress and blooming of the human soul.

Great leaders operate under this law. Through repulsion they send their most beloved warriors into the most dangerous fields of battle. They load their shoulders with the heaviest burdens, and if any pity arises within their nature, they repulse it. They see only the future victory, the victory of the Plan for which the group works; and they have maturity enough to sacrifice all that hinders the success of the Plan.

In the higher psychic domain this law continuously functions. The human soul develops pure Divine indifference and neutrality to contacts. He is neither flattered nor bribed by any contact. He stands as a server, ready to carry the command, even if the command is not pleasing to his personality. He repulses his personality interference, the interference of the elementals, and even the interference of his deep-seated and hidden commands.

The Law of Repulsion helps the leader and the members to stand in the light of their souls and relate to each other as souls and not as personalities.

In group life one must repulse the things that do not belong to him. He must repulse the praise which belongs to someone else and the honors which belong to someone else. He does not become interested in the message he is supposed to pass to someone else. If he is given money or things to distribute to others, he does not take them for himself. If he has to deliver a secret to someone, he does not try to know about it. If it is needed that he ignore certain people in public, he does it for their sake.

He repulses certain thoughts that come to him — for example, thoughts that tell him he is smarter than others, more advanced than others, better than others. He does not develop vanity and pride by nourishing such thoughts; he repulses them for the sake of his friends. He repulses positions or titles when he realizes that someone else can do better in that position.

The Law of Repulsion works on many levels, but it is always related to the group life, to group endeavor. This group law is a selective law. As we are told, "It works in seven directions." We are assuming that these seven directions are the Seven Rays. Through the Law of Repulsion the soul repulses the "atom," or the human soul, to go and find his own proper Ray and operate and unfold there.

Such an activity does not have the purpose of creating separatism but a symphony. Every note must find its own rightful place and sound at the right time. The "seven fathers" are the sevenfold chord composing the symphony. They are the Seven Great Rishis with Their seven representatives in our solar system.

To be able to use the Law of Repulsion, one must cultivate

1. Self-forgetfulness
2. Divine indifference
3. Discrimination
4. Compassion
5. Intuition
6. Holy detachment
7. Fearlessness

Self-forgetfulness is the ability to act and live on behalf of the One Life, on behalf of the Plan. Self-forgetfulness is the ability to hold back any personal interference in the group endeavor.

Whenever the personality self is demanding or forceful, it hurts the group and hinders its usefulness.

Self-forgetfulness is also the ability to turn off all glamors, illusions, and maya for the sake of the labor of the group.

Divine indifference is related to self-forgetfulness, but it is a slightly more advanced stage of the attitude of the Self in which the Self, "under any condition, remains unattached. The good and evil cannot disturb him and he neither praises nor condemns nor hates."[2]

Divine indifference is the ability to see the unfolding and progressing Spirit aspect without becoming confused by the phenomenal aspect under karmic stress and tribulation.

In Divine indifference one takes action only to assert the Spirit's progress. This virtue operates mostly under the direction of the First Ray and often appears to be extremely cruel, destructive, and painful. But this cruelty, destruction, and pain are not used to secure one's own or the group's interest, but as an act of sacrifice to liberate and release the enslaved souls from the prisons of materialism, selfishness, and totalitarianism.

Discrimination. Remember that virtues have octaves, and on each octave they present different manifestations. Discrimination on this octave is selection under the Plan and the Purpose, aided by the Law of Karma.

It is through intelligent and scientific discrimination that people are repulsed in order to let them find their proper center for unfoldment and service.

It is through intelligent and scientific discrimination that at the right time and in the right place a man is repulsed to make him go closer to his Soul. Discrimination at this level is not done from the viewpoint of the personality or the intelligence of the discriminator but in accordance with the Plan and Purpose. To have right discrimination one must know, through his own Intuition, the object of repulsion and his karma and then take the right steps for discrimination. On this level, right discrimination is a Divine agent.

Compassion is very important, especially in the reinforcing of the Law of Repulsion.

Compassion is not pity. Pity hinders the free action of the Spirit by focusing Its consciousness upon the personality reactions of the object. This is why pity is condemned.

Compassion is different. Compassion is the ability to fall in love with the soul aspect in spite of all negativity and impurity of the personality aspect and see the future achievements of that soul, in harmony with the Plan and Purpose. Compassion feeds the soul, the Spirit, and prepares a man to use the Law of Repulsion.

Intuition. Without Intuition, repulsion changes into rejection and separatism and creates various karmic complications. Intuition on this level is an ability to perform right action in harmony with the Plan, the Purpose, and the Karmic Laws.

It is possible that one cannot exactly formulate the reasons for his actions, but always he acts rightly. Intuition guides him even if he is not aware of all the intricate laws, forces, and energies in action at the time of his repulsion.

Intuition is used here not for personal enlightenment but to harmonize things with the Divine Plan and with the Divine Purpose.

Detachment, for one who is about to exercise the Law of Repulsion, is a very important virtue — detachment from not only one's physical, emotional, mental, and personal objects but also from the thought of *reward*.

In the early stages we try to detach from worldly objects. Then we work very hard to detach ourselves from our urges and drives, from our glamors and earthly desires, from our illusions and separatism. It is time now to learn how to detach from *ourselves*. This is an advanced stage on the Path. This is holy detachment.

One cannot act under the Law of Repulsion until he knows how to detach his Self from himself. As long as there is a "himself," the repulsion will be colored by the influence of the ego.

Detachment is the annihilation of the ego. The ego is you, plus the body with which you are identified.

Fearlessness is unshakable faith or intuitive awareness that nothing will be affected by your act of repulsion. Fearlessness will make it clear to you that the Law of Repulsion, in its essence, is an orchestration process.

In fearlessness you become a free server; you act in the freedom of Spirit, in the freedom of infinite Space.

Thus, through these seven virtues you carry out the Law of Repulsion. It is one of the great laws of group work. Real group work does not start until one is capable of working as a soul. This is easy to say, but every moment we see the effect of our personality, our ego.

Do not forget that the Law of Repulsion is related to objects, vehicles, or the interests of individuals. Under this law one repulses anything to be able to advance on the path of progress. This law is related to group life and group progress. Any repulsion must be done for the sake of the group and for the sake of the unit involved.

There are three sets of laws for our solar system. One set of laws emanates from light, from the physical Sun. These laws are directed and controlled by light, heat, and motion. They are related to individuals.

The second set of laws emanates from the Heart of the Sun, and these laws are controlled and directed by love, attraction, and repulsion. They are related to the group, to the Plan.

The third set of laws emanates from the Central Spiritual Sun. These laws are directed and controlled by will, thought, and purpose.

Under the first set of laws, the personality of the planet is controlled and directed, including the personality of living forms.

Under the second set of laws, the soul aspect of the planet and of man is controlled and directed. The soul aspect is a group-forming aspect and relates groups to groups. If these laws are not observed, we have wars and depressions. The main law in this second set of laws is the Law of Repulsion.

Repulsion is sometimes translated as hatred, rejection, and refusal. But its esoteric meaning is right relationship for the sake of the Plan.

Under the third set of laws, the Spirit aspect of the planet and of man is considered in relation to the solar system and galaxy. With these laws the progress of man toward the future and toward eternity is established.

Human groups and greater groupings, which are called Hierarchies, operate under the second set of laws.

The major intent of the Law of Repulsion is to create sensitivity within the group life to the pulsation of the Solar Heart.

Remember that this law is named after its *effect* and not after its causality. The effect is "repulsion," sensed and registered by the unit, but the intention of the repulsion is to find the center of the unit and direct it toward greater unfoldment and creativity.

This law works perfectly in the Hierarchy. A continuous repulsion goes on as the Ashrams form and reform, as the Initiates manifest Their deeper directions and needs, as the Hierarchies graduate from one level and come closer to the spheres of higher laws.

Interestingly enough, the difference between this Law of Repulsion and apparently similarly named laws is that the Law of Repulsion works in perfect understanding, love, and joy. This is the secret of why the repulsed units continue their cooperation with their former group as well as their new group — and become a bridge of cooperation between the group that repulsed them and the group that attracted them.

Practical implications of this Law can be seen in the formation of new groups by those who were parts of various former groups.

After formation and stabilization of a group, the Law of Repulsion begins to act. Members develop various characteristics which Nature must utilize by locating them in those groups where they can utilize their new unfoldments until new layers of their being are revealed. This is why a living group continuously radiates out, through the Law of Repulsion, those members who need new *centers*, new nuclei, and reorganizes itself as it receives new units from other groups.

Thus, in living groups there is no attachment, no fanaticism, and no refusal; but there is intuitive power as to the soul's direction.

We must also note here that the confusion, hatred, rejection, and cleavages seen in various groups are not necessarily the effect of the Law of Repulsion. The Law of Repulsion has no power over people who are not yet sensitive to their Souls. Those who are merged with their personality interests do not respond to the Law of Repulsion and thus wander not to find a center but to satisfy their personality glamors and interests.

This Law of Repulsion is seen operating in the creative thinking process. Once the man comes under the control of his Soul, his *thoughts* act under the Law of Repulsion. Thoughts are radiated out to form a galaxy around great visions and ideas. Then the relation between these visions and ideas is discovered, and all of them are rearranged around a more powerful and more inclusive vision or idea. This is how synthesis is achieved in thinking.

All accumulations and groups are formed under the Law of Repulsion.

At the beginning of the operation of this law, one feels the repulsion of the former center and the welcoming of the new center, yet unknown to him. One feels a joyful anxiety during this transition period, but the law operates firmly as one becomes more sensitive to the forces of attraction of the new center.

We must be careful not to confuse repulsion with detachment. They are two different things.

People think that the First Ray separates, divides, and builds a tower for itself. This is true if we are talking about the First Ray expressing itself through the personality. It is not true if the First Ray is expressing itself through the soul or through the Spiritual Triad.

When the First Ray manifests through our soul or spiritual nature, it works for synthesis. The Law of Repulsion is related to the Law of Synthesis. In appearance it rejects and separates, but in essence it synthesizes. Every separated grouping, when it starts unfolding its spiritual nature, is led to synthesis.

When one uses the force of detachment, he rejects certain elements to get rid of them, to secure his own progress. In the Law of Repulsion, the unit is repulsed for its own sake. Thus repulsion is based upon the foundation of selflessness, esoterically understood, and on the foundation of "losing oneself for the sake of others." Through the Law of Repulsion the university graduates are released to make them engage in their careers.

This is done on an individual and a group basis. "Groups" lose their identity to form a greater symphony with the "notes" repulsed. This is also called the Law of the Destroying Angel.

One can understand this when he remembers that at the Fourth Initiation the Solar Angel destroys the Temple and leaves the Spark free to choose a new center around which to revolve, letting the substance of the Chalice turn into Its wings.

The Angel standing with the Flaming Sword is the symbol of the First Ray. It prevents the reentry of those who were enjoying the pleasures of the garden which had been granted to them and makes them win the right to return to the garden on their own merit.

The Law of Transmutation is the path leading toward the Law of Repulsion.

"...the transmuting process, when effective, is superficially the result of outside factors. Basically it is the result of the inner positive nucleus of force or life reaching such a terrific rate of vibration, that it eventually scatters the electrons or negative points which compose its sphere of influence, and scatters them to such a distance that the Law of Repulsion dominates. They are then no more attracted to their original centre but seek another. The atomic sphere, if I might so express it, dissipates, the electrons come under the Law of Repulsion, and the central essence escapes and seeks a new sphere, occultly understood."[3]

It is through this law that the human soul is emancipated, continuously revolving around greater and higher centers, and on every spiral unfolds a part of his higher nature.

The Law of Repulsion is based on the principle of never ending progress and achievement.

The repulsed one passes on to a higher level of "education" or into a different field of influence where his hidden *potentials* bloom.

Notes:

1. Alice A. Bailey, *A Treatise on Cosmic Fire*, p. 1217.
2. *The Bhagavad Gita* 2:57, translated by author.
3. Alice A. Bailey, *A Treatise on Cosmic Fire*, p. 478.

14

Leaders and Crystallizations

One of the labors of the leader is to break crystallizations. We can define crystallizations as mental, emotional, and habitual forms; traditional, religious, philosophical, or educational forms. Every form with the tendency to separatism is a hindrance on the Path toward the Causeless Cause. Ways and means must be found to emancipate the Teaching crystallized or appropriated in any racial or national form or interest.

If we really penetrate into the essence of the agelong conflict between religions and traditions, we will find out that their origins are the same. But because of nationalization or personalization of the Teaching, instead of cooperative activities, armies emerged which stood against each other. If we investigate further, we will see that the leaders heading such armies forced people to engage in endless wars against each other.

This is how the One Teaching, instead of becoming a synthesizing factor, became a conflict-creating factor. People did not realize the oneness of the Teaching and separated it according to the patterns of their interests. Of course, this developed the human intellect and various techniques of fighting, but we have waited too long to come to our senses. We must try to discover the Teaching and present it in a way that neither nourishes separative interests, vanities, and pride nor is limited by them.

It is the time to engage ourselves in this labor of decentralization of the Teaching and of universalization of the Teaching. The Teaching must not be used for our racial, national, or political interests; rather it should be used

    a. To expand the consciousness of humanity and enable it to have contact with Higher Worlds

    b. To create greater and greater synthesis in humanity

    c. To make people strive toward perfection and harmony, or toward right relations with Nature and other human beings

    d. To control and master our bodies, their inertia, glamors, illusions, vanities, and ego

    e. To understand man and the Cosmos

We must not have Hindu teaching, Indian teaching, Tibetan teaching, Jewish teaching, Christian teaching, Zoroastrian teaching, and so on. We must have only the Teaching, unexploited by any nation, race, religion, or tradition.

The Teaching degenerates the moment it is nationalized and dressed in the traditions and superstitions of various nations. The Teaching must remain in its purity and stand above the separative interests of any national, racial, or traditional factions.

It is true that in all traditions the Teaching exists, but one must separate the built-up crust from the essence and use the essence as a path to discover the oneness of the Teaching. It is possible to put a fragrant oil into various bottles in various locations without being hindered to a degree that prevents you from seeing the same essence in all the bottles.

People took the Teaching and made it into religion and then divided religion into one thousand pieces. "This is this church; the other is that church," not just in Christianity but in all religions. Once religion is divided, it works against the highest interest of people and crystallizes the Teaching into exclusive parts.

Mulla Nasrudin told a beautiful story about how people handle an organized whole and destroy it: A few friends found a stork. They said, "Its beak is too long; its legs are too long.... Let us shape it and cut off whatever we do not think is proper." And they did. After they finished the operation, they very proudly released the bird to fly, but the bird was dead.

When the Teaching is chopped into millions of parts, it ceases to be a pure, healthy, living Teaching. It dies and serves separative interests — growing dogmas, doctrines, limitations, censures, and eventually inquisitions.

The Teaching of the Future is an all-embracing Teaching. It does not emphasize the parts which will form the synthesis. This Teaching is synthesized on the level of pure ideas, principles, and laws serving all. Any separative, antagonistic, or fanatical activities against any research and any effort to limit other people's freedom will eventually lead to a state of consciousness where the amputated religion, tradition, or teaching does not lead people on the path of perfection but serves only their material, separative interests.

It is very interesting to note that people often organize dialogues between religions, ideologies, and traditions to insist after the dialogue on the superiority of their own presentation, and the cleavage widens between them. Such dialogues must not be attended by people who

    a. Will use the dialogue to advertise themselves

    b. Are not searching for the essential unity behind the presentations or are not searching for a common denominator

One of the great obstacles on the path of discipleship is to study, meditate, and receive training only for one's own benefit, for one's own financial interest, for one's own personal reputation. This is one of the great obstacles that prevents the assimilation and clear, pure transmission of the Teaching. Personal interest and the Teaching cannot agree with each other.

People must learn to come to the Teaching not to draw personal benefits from it but to be trained to serve and transmit the Teaching. You see many students who come like gophers and penetrate into the Teaching to feel satisfied that they know more than others, to use the Teaching as if they were its source, and to make it a means to serve their financial, emotional, and egotistic needs. Such people usually distort the Teaching, translate it in terms of their narrow understanding, and always remain gophers, hiding themselves from the true light.

Some of these people are interested in the Teaching only for themselves; others as a business; others for racial or nationalistic interests. There are others who use the Teaching and come to the Teaching to meet people they need for their interests. They use the people they meet under the glamor of the Teaching. Once the Leader suspects such attitudes, he must, by subtle means, push them away from the Teaching.

The true attitude of a disciple must be: "Life is passing by. I realize that I must be useful to humanity. How can I be trained so that I offer myself to the service of the world and the service of the Higher Forces?" Such a disciple advances very fast, and he becomes one of the pillars of light instead of a gopher.

People were told that all that exists was created for their pleasure. Such an attitude exists among students. Nature is not created for man; man is created for Nature — as a part of a great mechanism. He is there to contribute to the Plan of the Great Life and understand the Purpose through serving that Purpose.

The same is true for the Teaching. The Teaching is not created for man to enjoy and use for his pleasure or self-interest. Man is destined to work according to the Teaching to serve the overall Plan and, through this service, find the path of self-perfection. Even self-perfection sounds selfish, but in its esoteric meaning the Self is One and the realization of this Self makes him perfect to relate, serve, and cooperate with all the members of the One Self.

Self-interest in the Teaching leads to dire consequences and hinders one's path for centuries. This is why real Teachers create obstacles on the path of unworthy students and make them occupy themselves with things on their own level. I remember my Teacher once rejected a well-known philosopher from participating in the classes. When I asked why such a learned man was rejected, he said briefly, "He came here to pump up his vanity."

The discipline of the path of perfection has one source. All the various disciplines, if they are related to the Higher Worlds, are essentially the same, but they have different names.

Once Mulla Nasrudin went to buy material for his wife's dress. When the shopkeeper was busy inside with some important work, the Mulla cut a piece off the cloth and put it in the pocket of his coat. When the shopkeeper came out, the Mulla said, "I will think about it, and later I will let you know if she wants to buy it or not."

The Mulla went to his wife and said, "Here is what you wanted, but be sure before you make a dress out of it that you dye it so that it has no resemblance to the bolt of material from which it was cut." The wife did not understand why.

She would have understood if we had told her that though the Teaching was given and each one needed to make use of it for his own need, instead each had dyed it in such a way that it did not bear any resemblance to the original source.

It is possible, and it is really unavoidable, to make the Teaching fit our level, but without changing its essence and color and keeping it related in some way to the Source of the Teaching. This is why it will be possible to keep the Teaching pure only by raising our consciousness to its Source and comparing what we have with the Source.

People must not try to belong to groups, religions, traditions, or teachings for the sake of belonging to them; but they must search for the Teaching beyond the borders of any church, group, religion, or teaching. When they asked Plato if he loved Socrates, he said, "I love him, but I love truth more than I love him." This will be the attitude of all those who want to understand the Teaching.

Vanities must not be encouraged, especially those vanities which are built on "mine and yours." Prostitution of the Teaching starts the moment when it is biased.

The Teaching leads to knowledge, to beingness, to creativity, and to unity. Knowledge is not religion only, but it is education, philosophy, science, art, and finance as well. All these fields have one source — the Teaching, the Light.

15

Leadership and Confusion

Some people think that no progress is achieved without confusion. This is not true. We do not need to confuse people to initiate a new vision. It is true that the new vision, the new knowledge, the new direction can be diametrically opposite to what was in existence; but the presentation of the new and the motive behind it can be so clear that people discard the old and receive the new without confusion.

In confusion the goal is not given, or the ways to it are so obscure that one does not even believe that a goal exists. In confusion, forces within you are "on strike." Carelessness and indifference are side effects of confusion.

Confusion causes paralysis in certain areas of our senses and nervous system. Many obstacles found on the path of our success, prosperity, and health originate from moments of recorded confusion. Clear the confusion, and the obstacles will disappear along with their effects.

In certainty, the goal is clear, though the ways may differ. People can reach a goal through different ways. But in confusion the goal does not really exist. When one has two goals opposing each other, he has no goal, and that is the same as inertia or depression. Even to have a wrong goal is better than to have no goal or contradictory goals.

In confusion, right and wrong are equal, or both do not exist.

Certainty requires vision, goal, honesty, beauty, health, nobility.

Confusion is an effort to destroy principles and ideas which people use to build their lives. Such an action is taken without presenting better principles and better ideas.

Confusion is not easy to impose at once upon the minds of people. It is promoted gradually through doubt and by undermining spiritual standards, moral principles, and values.

Doubt and confusion are either imported or manufactured by ourselves.

When a man has the ability to see his own reality but is unable to make his reality meet his needs and solve his problems, doubt develops. It is a doubt about reality, a doubt about his needs and problems, and a doubt about his ability to handle them. Doubt is a thoughtform which fluctuates between these three points and weakens all three by creating a confused relationship between them.

To clear any doubt from our minds we must clarify these three points:

1. Reality, as we accept it
2. Our needs
3. Our ability to handle the reality

Doubt generally is developed when reality, ability, and need are not clearly understood or explained.

Confusion is a state of mind in which these three points lose their meaning and the mind cannot discriminate between them. Thus reality seems to be the need, the need appears as ability, and ability becomes a distorted reality.

To take a man out of his confusion and doubt one must help him simplify his reality, his ability, and his need and understand them as they are. Daily he must be made to face his reality, ability, and need. The only thing you must do is to create for the person as many viewpoints as possible for these three objects. You must not approve or disapprove but ask questions and make him look at his objects from as many viewpoints as possible.

After the confusion and doubt are cleared away, the next thing to do is to generate a right motive in the man. If the reality, ability, and need are not handled with right motive, confusion and doubt appear once more, and this time with greater complications.

Right motive is the focus of a vision or a great idea which controls the activity of the mind, emotions, and body. Motive has an automotive power. Doubt and confusion cannot germinate again when the right motive is established in the heart.

The leadership in any department of human endeavor must be aware of the activities of the dark forces. Dark forces are those beings who, in the body, or out of the body try to create chaos, crimes, degeneration, and bloodshed.

All human endeavor is essentially oriented toward bringing in success, health, happiness, improvement, and spiritual perfection. But in all fields of human endeavor the dark forces are actively working to retard progress, cooperation, and synthesis.

One of the techniques that dark forces use is the technique of creating fear. Through fear the dark forces can create panic, disturbances, illogical activities, and crimes. But this technique does not always work when people stop and think, use their reason and logic, and try to reach their own conclusions.

This is why the dark forces use a new technique which is the technique of creating confusion and then fear.

Confusion breeds fear in such a way that the victim of confusion never suspects that he will fall into the hands of fear. In the technique of confusion, the victim is not warned, is not agitated, but fear is introduced into his consciousness like a posthypnotic suggestion, which eventually takes over the whole mechanism of the human being.

When fear is the result of confusion, it is the most deep-seated fear in the human heart. It is very difficult to bring a person out of this fear unless, first of all, his confusion is cleared away not only logically but also practically.

Fear created through confusion cannot be reached by logic. Such a fear rejects logic. It is a blind force activated by confusion. Thus, the instigator of confusion can manipulate the victim without the slightest opposition. Confusion knocks down the light of the intellect and makes people do irrational things.

Man uses the same technique to fish or to hunt animals. Confusion creates fear in them, which acts as a blind drive that pushes them into his traps. Our stock market uses the same fishing or hunting technique to confuse people, to create fear in them, and to manipulate them. Our news media is the victim of the technique of confusion.

The same technique is used in politics, in education, and in religion. Once confusion is aroused, the manipulators have a chance to harvest great benefits from the irrationality of people and their fears. At that time the bullion market can sell you gold at any price it wants because you are in fear and you are confused. When you are confused, you do not operate your mind correctly. Confusion paralyzes the thought mechanism momentarily or for an extended period of time.

We have confusion in our morals, in our ideals, in our goals and purposes. This is why deep in our heart it is fear that controls us, especially at moments of crisis.

I have read thousands of pages about the effects of marijuana. Some people positively condemn the use of marijuana. Others say it is beneficial. Both have their proofs and arguments. And no one who is confused can really know which position is right. The intelligent man in a state of confusion asks:

"What shall I do? Smoke marijuana or reject it?"

"Are these conclusions honest? Are they based on scientific proof?"

"Does one or both sides have ulterior motives or self-interests? Is there any politics behind this?"

Under such conditions one need not be a prophet to say that the use of marijuana will increase because people are confused.

In a state of confusion, the control of the person falls into the hands of blind urges and drives and of the pleasures of the body.

People are controlled and used once they are doped. A doped state of mind eventually develops fear and becomes very destructive. Notice the increasing crime rate.

We can see this technique used in many fields through radio, television, and various publications. The presentations are made in such a way that people cannot draw any conclusions, or people are faced with contradictory expressions and with doubtful data backing both expressions. Or the opposing viewpoints are presented in such a way that the average man is forced to accept both and goes crazy.

Some people develop double faces and, like an unconscious object, serve one or the other expression to secure their self-interest. Or they reject both expressions and live in a spirit of rebellion.

Confusion breeds fear, and when fear grows the opportunist feels satisfied because now he can control those who have developed fear. This is a technique also used by opportunists to pave the way for their dishonest motives.

When the mind is confused, it either acts mechanically by obeying the louder voice or it obeys the associative suggestions within itself. Associative suggestions are accumulated experiences in the subconscious mind which come and control the situation if they are associated with it. A confused mind refuses to accept new proposals, even if these proposals are given by one who really wants to help.

Confusion creates mass depression, mass suicide, and widespread crime, goallessness, and inertia. Most divorce cases are the result of confusion. Confusion is created by hypocrisy, by living other than by your convictions, other than by your commitments. Immorality creates confusion. Most movies are generators of confusion and lies. Imitation is also a technique of confusion.

The one who confuses people convinces them by literally saying, "That is not the way to go. This is not the way to go. There is no way to go."

When a man is trapped in confusion, he says, "The only way is the way I am telling you."

Confusion is the mixing of directions, principles, goals, reasons, and motives in such a way that they are in a state of conflict or a state of chaos.

When you are confused, try to find the underlying currents contributing to the confusion. Once you find the contributing currents, try to do the following:

1. Find the motives underlying the currents, the goals of the originators of the currents.

2. Try to see the way they are operating.

3. Study their presentation and find the exact foundations upon which their presentation is based. Very often you will not find a real foundation but only lies.

4. Study the opposite currents.

5. After you compare them do one of the following:

    a. Support one of them.

    b. Make your own conclusions, finding beneficial points from each of them.

    c. Choose your own direction based on the following criteria:

— The most beautiful

— The most beneficial for the greatest number of people

— The direction that promises greater moral discipline

— The direction that does not encourage separative interests

But after doing all this, keep yourself alert because those who confuse have earthly, cunning wisdom and knowledge. If you are not watchful, you may be trapped in their new inventions.

In the history of humanity the confusion technique is always used when people want to achieve totalitarian power. But the most interesting point is that confusion is like the mythological fish who drank the whole lake with great enthusiasm and found out that it precipitated his own destruction.

Confusion is also created in religious and psychic fields. People everywhere are channeling "higher powers" and broadcasting their experiences. Most of these messages are shallow, funny, or contradictory. People are speaking in tongues, and tremendous chaos is created in the minds of the average person. Only the healthy ones found an escape from this trap by rejecting all that is given by such lower psychics.

A psychic came and told me, "You are very important in the eyes of God."

"Well," I said, "I know that two thousand years ago God loved the world so much that He gave His Son to save each of us."

"But," he said, "you are special."

"Well," I said, "all of His creation, every part of it is special."

"But," he said, "I received a message to tell you how important you are."

"I would not be more than what I am now. On the contrary, I would be less and do less if I went into that vanity."

A week later, another psychic called me and said, "The Master told me to tell you that all you are doing is wrong."

"Give my gratitude to him and say that if I cannot do better, the next thing he should do is come and do things better himself."

This is the situation. They read your aura and your past lives, and the goal is to create confusion in you. After you are confused, you fall victim to the hands of those who are using such psychics and channels.

We have the same technique of confusion promulgated by the many different approaches to the teaching of metaphysics, health, nutrition, meditation, psychism, and so on. The dark forces at this time are not attacking any technique or teaching. Instead, they are taking a technique or a teaching and distorting it and slowly creating a diametrically opposite teaching to confuse people. Once people are confused, they reject the teaching — to the great satisfaction of the instigators of the confusion.

There is also the defamation technique which destroys the possibility of a vision for the new generation. For example, if a great man, because of his ideas and leadership, is standing as a vision for future generations, the instigators of the confusion take his name, dig into his personality life, mix reality with unreality, and present a picture of him which is contrary to his moral code thus damaging his name and creating disrespect toward him. In this way our youth is raped of its vision and hence of the possibility of striving and improvement.

This confusion technique is even used to destroy the influence of great art, music, and literature. For example, I saw a drama about Goethe's Faust distorted in such a terrible way that I never wanted to read that book again. The same thing is done to other great literature of the world.

We see the confusion technique used in many conventions, retreats, and seminars where contradictory viewpoints are presented to the audience with the same excitement and emphasis. At the end of the seminar the audience is more confused than before. Thus, in the name of culture and wisdom, the confuser achieves a great success in diffusing and confusing the minds of the audience. Such an audience will very probably lose interest in a subject which only creates confusion, uncertainty, and headaches.

You can find the same confusion about the subject of meditation. Every teacher defines meditation differently and has a different approach and method for meditation. Those who hate meditation are mostly those who tried several methods and then, seeing that many forms of meditation exist, rejected it wholesale.

What we need is certainty, clarity, and simplicity. Confusion has the intention of manipulating you, of weakening you, of preventing you from growing, and of taking your freedom away from you.

Confusion is a method of attack on those principles or ways which will bring greater freedom to humanity. When the issue is really important and is urgent, then you see forces mobilizing themselves to confuse the minds of people and run the show. It is better for you to know less but be sure of what you know and your knowledge. It is better for you to know less about abstract metaphysics but be sure about your simple contact with God through your prayers.

Confusion eventually weakens and disappears when you cultivate straight-knowledge, intuition and sensitivity, and when in the darkest hours of your life you stick with the concepts of Beauty, Goodness, Righteousness, Joy, and Freedom.

We see the technique of confusion working in the musical field. Rock music, disco, acid and punk rock music and their other sisters and brothers are there to create confusion — confusion in your musical sense, distortion in your mental field, distortion in the natural arrangement of the cells and atoms of your brain, distortion in those areas of your mental field which are oriented and polarized toward great visions, creativity, service, labor, and striving for greater achievements.

These fields are distorted by confusing music, and the followers of such music find themselves less and less interested in achieving moral and spiritual heights and serving humanity in its effort to solve the world's problem; they sink into apathy, goallessness, drugs, and they reject the values needed for the survival of humanity.

The same confusion is contrived and sold widely in the field of color and painting. So-called modern art is presenting us with confusing forms, forms that distort our sense of beauty and create a deep confusion of artistic values. The same confusion is proliferated in certain movements and dances, such as when you see girls and boys throwing themselves to the ground, rolling, screaming, and moving chaotically. Nature is geometrical, measured, arithmetical, ordered, rhythmic, and cyclic; but here you have movements and motions that are the reflections of chaotic emotions, thoughts, and inner conflicts.

Art has certain high aims: to sublimate, to uplift, to expand the human consciousness, and to create harmony and certainty.

People may defend such confused arts through their own philosophy, but one must wait and do years of research to find out that the exponents and followers of such music, dances, and paintings gradually lose their health and happiness. They lose their friends, and without a science of right human relationship they slowly descend into depression, hopelessness, failure, and even suicide.

Watch the result of such confusion in your life, and you will have the answer. You can render a great service to people when you disperse confusion and bring in certainty. Certainty is alignment of the forces, centers, and fires of your system. Certainty draws energy from your Soul. Certainty impresses people and creates in them trust, confidence, and faith toward you.

A leader must be very careful not to create confusion with his teaching, speech, behavior, and relationships. He must stand in sincerity, honesty, openness, and readiness to communicate with simplicity and love.

Some Teachers consciously use an apparently similar technique, called the balancing technique, which does not confuse you but brings you to your senses and creates balance in your thinking or behavior. Once this balance is established, you begin to think deeper. The confusion technique does not create balance. It is a state of mind which is very close to dizziness, an uncomfortable turbulent situation from which you want to escape.

The balancing technique is quite different. For example, if you are really lost in one philosophy, the Teacher presents you with another philosophy. Its study will show you that yours is not the only philosophy. Your Teacher can also present different subjects to expand your consciousness but not confuse you.

Also, in the balancing system, the Teacher presents you with two different viewpoints and leaves you free to choose, whereas in the confusion technique the freedom of choice is suspended in you.

In all countries, leaders have used a technique to control people. We call it the technique of humiliation. Once a person is humiliated, it is very easy to control and use him for the advantage of persons, groups, or government. It is a very subtle method which is used in politics, in education, in the media, in the arts, in science, in religion, and in economics.

For example, to control and use a woman, people humiliated her. They told her that she must not have equal rights. They told her that she was inferior in intellect. They exploited her body, her sex. In most movies she played roles that degraded or humiliated her.

A woman was belittled to control her and to use her. When women revolted against such a humiliation, the leaders of exploitation changed their technique and found sneakier ways to further humiliate a woman. They said to her, "Your husband must not dominate you; he has no right to expect obedience from you. You can drink, dope, and prostitute yourself. You can easily divorce;

you can come home any time you want and let your husband cook and take care of the children. You can start sex at thirteen, fourteen, or fifteen years of age, and there is nothing wrong with it."

And the woman did all these things and humiliated herself with illegitimate children and abortions . . . and found herself trapped in various crimes . . . and called it "woman's liberation."

On the contrary, those who wanted to free the woman are those who wanted to make her the best mother, the best wife, or the best executive, lawyer, doctor, or politician, with dignity and honor.

Once you make a woman believe that she has no value, she has no value and she will give up being a value.

I was in a restaurant late at night, and two young people were sitting close to my table. The boy said, "I love you, and I want to make love with you."

"I love you too," said the girl, "but my intention is not first to make love because I want to know you better. Later I want to marry."

"Well, I don't want to marry, but I like to have fun."

"I need time to think about it."

I said to myself, "Things are going well. Let me see what else the boy is going to try."

Then the boy looked at the girl and said, "Well, you are not as beautiful as I expected you to be. Especially your eyes are weird, but I love you."

I thought, "He is playing smart."

"Well," said the girl, "then let me go."

"Go, then, but no one will love you as I do."

The girl left and went out to her car but came back with tears in her eyes and sat by him and said, "I know you love me."

And the boy hugged her and kissed her. Three minutes later the boy took her in his car and disappeared.

This is the way the modern opportunists win in any field of human endeavor. They belittle and humiliate you by cutting your salary, by not paying attention to you, by making you feel that you are nothing, and then they use you the way they want. When they humiliate you, they make you dependent on their actions, judgments, and attention.

Of course, the reverse action slowly builds up, but opportunists find different ways to humiliate you.

I once had a neighbor who wanted to buy another neighbor's home in which three brothers were living. All his visits and advice did not bring him success. Eventually he found a way. He visited again and pretended he was using opium and encouraged them to use it once, twice .... The next week he visited them with a "famous" girl who stayed there trying opium and other drugs. This continued for six months.

Then one day he saw me at the gate and said, "I know I am going to buy that property and at a very reasonable price ...."

"Well," I said, "you tried hard."

"Those who do not know the value of their property must not own it."

"Right."

"I will buy yours, too, if you want."

"Well, I will tell you something. No one can enjoy things that he gets by dishonest means."

He gave me a look and went away.

The boys became heavily involved with opium and were not able to pay the mortgage. The neighbor loaned them money at a high interest and the loan multiplied. Eventually the three brothers thought it would be wise to sell the property to their *benefactor*!

You cannot conquer anyone unless you weaken him first, or humiliate and dishonor him and make him lose faith in himself.

Criticism and various other forms of attack have the same basic motives. When one is beaten, criticized, debased, and belittled, his first reaction is: "I need someone to help me, to protect me, to support me." After such a thought follows the act of surrender. Naturally, the criticizer or the one who tried to humiliate you pretends that he is the one who can restore you if you become his slave.

Many, many people cannot find any other way than to be a comfortable slave.

We obey those who have power. The demonstration of this power is a subtle attack on you to tell you that you are nothing if you do not obey, and only a powerful one can uplift you if you admit your weakness.

You can see this technique in operation in religious institutions when, for example, the minister starts his sermon as follows: "You are lost in your sins; the fire of hell is already waiting for you, you miserable sinners. Come and repent . . . ." And people turn into sheep.

Are there not other ways to elevate people out of their level and make them beautiful instead of humiliating them? But humiliation makes people sheep, and sheep do what the wolf wants them to do.

This technique is an old-age technique still in operation but in the Future it will slowly disappear as people develop more faith in their own inner, essential Divinity. Then they will challenge each other not because of their weakness but because of their beauty and virtues.

Many civilizations failed, age after age, because no one can build a lasting civilization on a foundation of humiliation.

To find out such things for yourself, observe life and human relations. When you see something interesting, first observe it for a while and think about your observation. If you immediately analyze it, you will reach the wrong conclusion because you will translate it through your older logic. But if you observe it a while, you will have a chance to use new viewpoints, new logic, or a higher plane logic.

Someone asked me one day, "When I tell my girlfriend that she is beautiful, smart, and creative, she hates me. Why is that?"

The answer I gave him was: If you tell a person that she is beautiful, smart, and creative when she is not, you are belittling yourself and insulting her. In other words, you are flattering her. Before you tell her that she is beautiful you must believe that she is beautiful, that she is smart, that she is creative. Then if she is, she will enjoy your remarks about her. When she does not believe that she is beautiful, she will think you are flattering her and she will reject you. She does not have faith in you since you did not see what she really is. She does not want you to know her weaknesses, but she also does not want you to lie to her."

You can say exactly what your girlfriend is, and this will not hurt her if she sees that you accept her in your love. But if you say she is beautiful when she is not, and that you love her because of her beauty, she will think, "This man is fooling me. He is flattering me. He does not love me in reality because he knows I am not beautiful!"

Be grateful to people but do not praise them until you see that they feel worthy enough to be *appreciated.*

Once a girl told me that she was trash. Her inferiority complex was so deep that I did not dare to attack it. But I kept talking, and then a smart idea came to my mind. I said, "I feel hungry, so let me fry some potatoes and let us eat." We went to the kitchen and I took a potato and tried to peel it.

"My goodness," she said, "you can't do it that way. Watch me and do it this way." And she very skillfully peeled the potatoes. I really admired her with my eyes and manners. Then she prepared the table and made a salad, and we sat down to eat.

"You know," I said, "you peel potatoes much better than I do. But I know that next time you come, you will see that I will do better."

"Well," she said, "I bake the best bread."

"You do?"

"Yes."

"Can you bake bread for me?" And she kept herself really busy for a while and made the best bread.

I said, "This is delicious. I love this bread."

"You are the only man who appreciated me."

"Well, I can tell you this bread is delicious and you peel potatoes better than I do — and I am so grateful to you."

The face, the look, the behavior of the girl changed in one visit. I did not flatter her. I did not affirm her opinion about herself as being trash, but I appreciated her.

This is one of the ways to free people from many kinds of slavery.

There is another factor within the human being which inspires greatness in every individual. This factor is the Transpersonal Self, the Solar Angel.

The Solar Angel stands within you as an ideal, as a vision. Often you wonder why you are not as beautiful as you wanted to be, as you thought you were. This is because in rare moments you had an identification with your Solar Angel and glimpsed a vision of greatness, but in the next moment you came back to your normal level. Thus the existence of the Solar Angel within you gives you a chance to compare what you are with what you can be. The presence of the Solar Angel within you makes you strive toward the ideal that you experienced in the few moments when you were consciously elevated. Such experiences give you a conviction that you can be great; because you were great once, you can do it again.

The existence of the Solar Angel within you creates polarity, direction, and motion. Any degree of contact with the Solar Angel inspires you to strive toward greatness. If you are physically inclined, you search for physical and material greatness; if you are mentally inclined, you look for intellectual greatness. But when you become spiritually inclined, you search for spiritual greatness. The contact makes you move, experience, and find your own way toward real greatness.

A similar effect is produced when an individual comes in contact with a Great One. Like a magnet the Great One creates a polarization within you toward your Real Self. You again have a high degree of polarization when you contact real beauty in any form. Thus all of Nature inspires us to transcend ourselves.

Self-condemnation is a technique suggested by the forces of darkness. A man who continuously condemns himself loses his respect for himself and eventually lives a degenerate life.

Self-condemnation is a terrible kind of self-hypnotism. When you fill yourself with such suggestions, you will always feel stupid and confused when events occur in your life that associate you with the moment you condemned yourself. It is also a great disrespect to your Inner Divinity.

If you do some research you will find that your failures are accumulated expressions of your moments of self-condemnation in the past. Your failures are directly connected to your self-condemnation. When your faith in yourself is destroyed by self-condemnation, you are like a car without gas.

Remember the mantram:

> *More radiant than the sun,*
> *Purer than the snow,*
> *Subtler than the ether,*
> *Is the Self,*
> *The spirit within my heart.*
> *I am that Self.*
> *That Self am I.*

When you begin to respect yourself, your physical, emotional, and mental elementals will start respecting you and synchronizing with your higher strivings. These elementals only obey you when you affirm your self-respect, or when you build a self-image that is beautiful. I am not referring to any kind of showing off or imitation.[1]

Man lives far below what he is or is going to be. You must live in the world as you are inside. You must bring out the greatness that you are in your being and live in a way that greatness reaffirms itself in all your relationships.

People live in ways that are less than what they are. They identify themselves with this lesser image, and then they act under its control.

People think that you can be anything in your outer relationships. This is esoterically wrong because when others have a lesser image about you, they will deal with you according to the lesser image. Then their opinion of you will impress your aura and make you act as they think you should act.

If you are a king within yourself, live like a king so that you do not have a strange thoughtform imposed upon you by others.

This is why we are told *to shine our light*.

Notes:

1. See also *The Mystery of Self-Image*.

16

Vigilance

Vigilance is a great virtue of leaders of the spiritual path. It is sometimes called the crown of the warrior. Each jewel in the crown is an eye which is vigilant, day and night, on objective and subjective planes, and which registers clearly those currents which are in harmony with the Plan and those which disturb the Plan.

Thus the eyes in the crown report to the crown information from not one direction but many directions. The crown uses this information as a whole. The crown relates all information, synthesizes it, and takes right action.

In the Teaching of the Great Ones we are told that there is a difference between vigilance, observation, and watchfulness.

Observation is related to objects, events, people, signs, their movements, causes, effects, motives, destinations, significances. All these are observed from a viewpoint to know the condition of life and find better ways and means to serve and to uplift.

Watchfulness is related to one's own self. One tries to be awake in all conditions to protect his life and the life of others, to carry on his responsibilities, to secure control over his thoughts, words, and actions.

Vigilance synthesizes these two actions or operations. In addition, vigilance observes and keeps watchful from the viewpoint of spiritual values to harmonize the life to the pull of the Cosmic Magnet.

Thus observation, watchfulness, and vigilance are related to mind, heart, and spirit.

On the path to Ashrams one must develop all three of these qualities because this path is an ever-changing path, and the traveler is in a different state of consciousness with his every next step.

It is interesting that with vigilance, prayer is also mentioned. Prayer is the effort to keep the Higher Guidance continuous on the path of perfection.

Vigilance is not surface observation, but is a state of alertness and awakeness in all directions. Vigilance grows through our unfoldment and experiences. Man is mostly asleep or half asleep. He does not have full consciousness. Most of the time he is aware of life in general only ten to fifteen percent. Life flows by him, and he is not conscious of the events, energies, forces, and messages coming from various sources.

Vigilance starts on the physical plane when man starts to protect himself or others from accidents, to protect his or others' possessions, land, rights, etc. He is immediately aware if there are forces against his or others' security, positions, and rights.

Eventually the field of alertness expands to the emotional world. Man is alert toward his emotions and the emotions of others. He sees the results and the effects of his emotions, and eventually he alerts himself to the slightest negative emotions coming either from his or other people's nature. Vigilance on the emotional plane saves a great amount of time, energy, money, and life.

Here, vigilance means to have a sharp sensitivity and discrimination toward all those emotions which are dangerous for one's body, heart, and mind or dangerous to the welfare of others.

This vigilance also extends to subtle levels. A vigilant man registers emotional waves coming from various sources. He discriminates between them and takes action to prevent them from entering his aura, or he welcomes them if they are constructive.

Emotional vigilance is also exercised subjectively on the astral plane. Astral entities and astral forces can easily sneak in, ruin our character and principles, and involve us in unending problems. Vigilance protects the subject from such an astral danger and teaches him how to fight degenerative forces and glamors on the astral plane.

Vigilance does not end on the emotional plane. It extends to the mental plane. It is on the mental plane that true vigilance begins to function. Man develops mental alertness. His observation reaches a very keen stage where he reads minds, translates thoughts, penetrates into motives, and stands guard over all those thoughts and thoughtforms which are contrary to the welfare of the whole man, to the welfare of those around him, and to the welfare of humanity as a whole. He promptly rejects destructive, ugly, and criminal thoughts and does not let them lay their eggs in his mind.

One of my Teachers used to say that a criminal, ugly, or destructive thought is like a flea or a termite. You must not let one of them enter your home because they multiply so quickly and so abundantly that you will have a very hard time cleaning them away.

Vigilance guards the mental plane and does not let any flea or termite enter in.

Vigilance sees the motives and intentions of people and takes action to protect himself.

Vigilance is more important than the weapons you have in your hand. Vigilance makes you aware of where the enemy of your soul is.

After a man develops mental vigilance, he clearly watches all that goes on in his emotional and physical planes and all that goes on in the physical, emotional, and mental planes of the world.

There is another degree of vigilance which is intuitional vigilance. At this stage mental vigilance — as the labor of analysis, observation, reasoning, and logic — is surpassed, and man has a certain light in his aura which automatically rejects, accepts, destroys, or harmonizes all impressions coming toward him.

Intuition is vigilance itself. It is the state of an awakened man, a totally conscious man who is aware of all that transpires on the lower three planes of man and the world and who automatically controls all influences, actions, and reactions.

Intuitive vigilance makes a man a guard. He guards humanity, and in the name of human welfare he engages himself in the most complicated battles of the world, not only on the physical plane but also on the astral and mental planes, where he carries on a heroic battle for the welfare of humanity.[1]

Vigilance is the foundation. It is the sword and shield of the warrior.

No one can achieve vigilance if he does not refine and develop his senses on all planes and build continuity of consciousness between the lower mind, the higher mind, and the Intuitional Plane.

From childhood vigilance must be cultivated. Children must be trained to be alert on all occasions through games and life events. They must be alert to

- The sacredness of Life

- Beauty, Goodness, Righteousness, Joy, Freedom, and unity

- Limitless expansion of consciousness and limitless unfoldment of the human soul toward perfection

- The fatherhood of God

- The immortality of the human soul

If these five principles are protected with vigilance from various unseen and seen sources, humanity will enter its Golden Age.

Evil is also vigilant. It works along destructive lines, but its vigilance does not pass beyond the mental plane.

Those who are vigilant on the Intuitional Plane watch the steps and activities of the enemies of mankind. They detect all their secret paths and eventually catch them in their own self-made traps. This is how evil destroys itself. Every force that is acting against Beauty, Goodness, Righteousness, Joy, Freedom, and unity is destined to perish as humanity develops vigilance on higher and higher planes.

There is a beautiful passage in the proverbs of King Solomon which reads:

"Do not envy evildoers nor be jealous of the wicked. For there shall be no future for evil men, and the lamp of the wicked shall be put out. My Son, fear the Lord and give good counsel; and meddle not with the fools. For their calamity shall come suddenly; and who knows the end of their years?"[2]

Vigilance can be developed by concentration exercises, through meditation, through a life of sacrificial service, through spiritual refinement, and through contact with higher realms. As one becomes more spirit and less matter, he increases in vigilance; he becomes more aware, more awake.

Everything against our vigilance must be avoided, such as

- Waste of physical, emotional, and mental energy
- Drugs
- Marijuana
- Smoking
- Alcohol
- Meat
- Smog and fumes of poisonous gases
- Other chemicals which dull the consciousness

- Hatred
- Fear
- Greed
- Irritation
- Dishonesty
- Separatism
- Exploitation
- Ignorance
- Lack of rest and vacation
- Certain music — rock and roll, hard rock, disco, and the like
- Flashing colors
- Unsteady light
- Certain currents of energy
- Excessive watching of television
- Heavy noise from traffic, electric machines, or airplanes
- Abnormal sexual relationships and excessive desire
- Polluted imagination
- Ugly conversation
- Lack of solemnity

These are causes which slowly carry us into sleep. They obscure our consciousness. We lose our alertness on physical, emotional, and mental planes, and we sink into drowsiness and torpor.

Once in a monastery I saw three sticks each three feet high. They were near the gate of the Temple. On one of them was written "pain," on the second was "suffering — death," on the third one was "danger." I asked a Teacher, "Why are these sticks here? When are they used and why?"

"Don't you see?" he said. "They are used all over the globe to prod the cattle on."

"Which cattle?"

"Those who fall asleep on the Path, those who entered the Temple without themselves knowing the taste of these sticks — these sticks kept them awake and vigilant."

"Can't humanity be awakened in a better way?"

"Unfortunately, no. At least for a time man needs these sticks, and he uses them continuously to awaken himself. There will come a time when man will have ever-increasing joy. When he awakens . . . yes . . . when man awakens from his sleep in matter."

I remembered these three sticks. I tasted them all through my life. Whenever I made mistakes, whenever I went against my conscience, whenever I bypassed beauty, these sticks were there. Only in a vigilant battle for perfection do you bypass these three sticks.

The whole process of evolution is a process of awakening. The more you are awake, the more you are your True Self. The more you are awake, the more you have control over your vehicles and your senses. The more you are awake, the more you are in harmony with the principles of Beauty, Goodness, Righteousness, Joy, Freedom, and unity. All achievements on all levels are the result of vigilance.

In vigilance you are striving. You are using your willpower, your sense of direction, your sense of unity and universality.

The crown of the warrior has many jewels. Each jewel is a sense for contact with the Existence. Each jewel in the crown is an eye.

Notes:

1. See also *Other Worlds*, Ch. 24, "Battle and the Subtle Worlds."
2. Proverbs 24:19-22

17

World Leadership

Leadership is always related to an inner guidance. One cannot be a leader if there is no one who guides him. All one's knowledge and experience fall short in comparison to the need and to world problems. The leader needs a telescope or a microscope to decide what to do, and the telescope and microscope are the inner guidance.

The first guidance comes from the Inner Watch. When the leader shows greater dedication and faces greater problems, the guidance comes to him from the Hierarchy via his Master or Soul. If he becomes a World Leader, such as a Buddha or a Christ, his guidance comes from the "Father." Thus leadership is always related to inner guidance.

Our Inner Watch, our Teacher, not only advises us but also warns us. A great leader is known not only for what he does but primarily for what he does not do.

When the leader advances and becomes conscious in the Subtle Worlds, he begins to see dangers and opportunities facing him. If some people are planning to disturb the leader or to trap him in certain ways, he can see their plan actualized in the Subtle World, and he acts accordingly to protect himself or his work or to make them fail in their efforts.

He also sees the opportunities, and on the physical plane he takes steps to benefit from them. The actualization of the dangers in the Subtle World comes from the thoughts and feelings of those who do the planning, but the actualization of the opportunities in the Subtle World comes from the Inner Watch, Who sends him visions and inspiration to alert him and make him sensitive to the opportunity.

The higher you can go in the Subtle Planes, the better leader you can be because your guidance comes from higher sources.

The real leader depends on all his experiences, resources, and powers, but he is also sensitive to the Leading Hand from the Inner World. Once he builds the link between himself and the inner guidance, he is a leader.

So-called democracy is a failure. A leader cannot be elected by those human beings who cannot yet see beyond their noses or by those who have separative interests. The real leader elects himself by the power he receives from the Inner Worlds. No one elected Zoroaster, Akbar, Buddha, Moses, Christ. They elected themselves by the power given to them from the Higher Worlds.

People cannot elect a leader. A person who is going to be a leader by election will fail if he does not have the Inner Contact. Thus in so-called democratic countries, nations are led by the consciousness and desires and level of average people. The blind lead the blind, and reforms and changes become extremely difficult, especially when they hurt the interests of certain parties.

Pollution cannot be stopped because people are making money from pollution.

The masses impose their own measures on their elected leaders and make them serve their interests, instead of serving the guidance of Higher Worlds. If there is no link between a leader and the Higher Worlds, that leader will either be the slave of the masses or he will exploit the masses for his own pleasures.

The signs that a leader has a link with the Higher Worlds are as follows:

— He works for the whole, not for the parts.

— He leads people toward moral perfection.

— He eliminates all those activities which cultivate in the masses irresponsibility, indifference toward their duties, license, crime, wrong human relations, separatism, and self-interest.

— He organizes the group or nation in such a way that he guarantees the survival of the people.

— He organizes education to help expand the consciousness and transform human nature.

— He fights against all those actions which endanger the health, prosperity, and security of people.

— He watches all the movements of the courts so that they not only judge righteously but also organize the ways and means and conditions to help people not to fall into crimes.

— He organizes institutions to promote physical health, moral health, mental health, and spiritual health.

Above all these things, the leader exemplifies all that he wishes to see in the people he leads.

Eighty percent of the population of the democratic countries do not really know for whom they are voting. Their votes are bought by an intelligently prepared advertisement or propaganda. People really have one or two choices, but they have no way of knowing the person for whom they are voting.

Pseudo leaders push their people toward dishonesty. People feel that to satisfy the dishonesty of the leader is a crime, but becoming dishonest toward the leader's dishonesty is for them the only way to protect themselves from the danger of the leader's dishonesty.

When people live in such an atmosphere, they feel inner conflict, fear, and confusion. Under wrong leadership, people eventually degenerate. The more the false leadership imposes its will on people, the quicker their degeneration because they try to find all kinds of dishonest ways to escape from the power of the leadership. This leads to inner defeat. When one defeats his conscience, his inner dignity, he falls from the path into massive destruction.

The real leader provides *conditions* in which people do not attempt to be dishonest. These conditions are not created by imposition, fear, or threat, but by security alone. People need security to be honest. In insecure conditions people have no choice, and they turn against themselves and against the pseudo leader the weapons of dishonesty — which seems to them the righteous way to act.

Friendship, cooperation, and leadership are based upon the foundation of gratitude and righteousness.

When gratitude departs from our hearts and righteousness dies in our soul, friendship and cooperation vanish.

It is important to cultivate the sense of gratitude and righteousness in those especially who are striving toward a greater service.

But to have gratitude you must realize how much you received, how much you were guided, and how much you were protected in your friendship and cooperation. If you cannot see this, you will not be ready to feel grateful.

To have the sense of righteousness is not easy. You must have a great honesty to see how much you owe to your friends, teachers, parents. Did you pay for all that was given to you? Did you pay back for the protection and blessings? Did you pay back for the wisdom and love given to you especially during your days of darkness?

How can you be righteous when you deny all that was done for you? How can you be righteous when you deny all that was given to you?

One of the greatest self-defeats is denial of the help *given* to you. And the greatest failure in your past is when you forget the things done for you.

Your denial and your attitude of ingratitude will continue with those whom you will meet. You will relate and you will use them until your ego and vanity are satisfied. Then you will leave them and search for new victims.

This will lead you slowly to loneliness, loaded with moral debts, and your artificial ornamentation will melt away.

Before you reach such a stage of defeat, remember those who enlightened you and protected you, and express gratitude to them even with your tears.

After you taste the sweetness of your gratitude you will understand the meaning of righteousness, and you will turn back and cooperate with those who serve humanity.

The real leader puts standards and creates conditions for people to follow. He does not follow after people. If people lead the leader, the leader serves their urges and drives and helps them to degenerate.

The leader stands as the representative of a plan, of a principle. He prepares those people who will help others to polarize themselves toward new standards, to strive for new achievements, and to conquer those parts of their nature which remain as yet unconquered.

When people choose the leader they want him to please them or they will make him resign, until they find one who will facilitate their degeneration. People find many ways to disguise such a thought, but history shows that moral degeneration is the result of wrong leadership, especially of leadership which is voted for and put into position by the will of the people. Hundreds of nations are experiencing such a downfall of morals and an increase in crimes, but they are not seeing the cause.

The leader sets the standards; he lives by them and creates those educational and disciplinary systems which make people understand, accept, and follow the standards. Leadership is like an educational process. In a university we have standards; those who want to graduate must meet the standards. Those who do not meet the standards of the university have no way of graduating. If they change their courses or even the university, they have to meet different standards. Life must be organized to meet the standards of leadership. Leadership is authority, and authority plans those steps which will carry the human masses to the path of perfection.

After frustrating failures, humanity will finally demand leaders. They will be tired of playing with votes. They will see that a pseudo democracy was exploiting them. They will see that it was talking about freedom but was imposing itself through power, money, and propaganda in order to secure the election of the one who would serve not principles but various interests.

People argue about personal freedom and personal privacy as if they had personal freedom and privacy. The way life is going at the present will very soon prove that people have no freedom and no privacy at all, in spite of all the propaganda about democracy.

Any real leader who tries to set high standards for the people will have the same fate as all those who tried to improve the spirit of humanity. Why was Moses rejected; why did he break the tablets of the Commandments? Why did people crucify Christ and hundreds of other leaders as well? Because they were real Leaders and they had standards!

There are wrong methods and there are right methods to make people follow standards. The wrong methods run on the line of imposition, fear, punishment, and threats. The right methods are education, healing, and preparation. Not a single person would reject spiritual transformation unless he were ignorant, sick, or insane. If he is in one of these states, then he needs education, medicine, and psychotherapy. Then he will accept the principles and work for them.

Totalitarianism must be clearly defined. Totalitarianism is a system by which one person or a group of people use all the resources of the whole for his own or their own private interests. Leadership is the opposite of totalitarianism. The leader's time, energy, and possessions are used to serve all people, to help all people reach a healthier, happier, purer, more enlightened, and more victorious life. Christ said something which fits here. He said, "Take and eat. This is My Body . . . ."

Real leadership wants people to assimilate the plan, the standard, and the vision it presents as a challenge and as a way that cannot be avoided if one wants to grow and become mature.

Pseudo democracy has allowed people to be prostitutes, to have abortions, to open gambling businesses, to sell pornographic literature and movies . . . and many other things.

Hundreds of years ago the prophet Nathan stood in front of King David and said, "You are wrong." At the present, even ministers are afraid to open their mouths about the transgressions of their congregation. The majority rules and when the majority rules people prepare the way for massive destruction.

Every leader must have guidance from Higher Worlds. Christ once said, "It is not I Who is doing all these things, but the Father Who is within Me." This is true Leadership. Real Leaders make the will of the Higher Forces manifest through themselves.

Leadership and responsibility go together.[1] Without responsibility, you do not have a leader. To have responsibility means not to create hindrances on the path of evolution for any living form, but, on the contrary, to try to create those conditions in which every living form will be able to manifest its beauty and fulfill its destiny. When the leadership violates the rights of the life, growth, or unfoldment of any living form, he is an imposter not a leader.

Leadership does not create those conditions in which you lose your time, energy, money, or opportunity to unfold; rather it creates those conditions in which you use your time, energy, and money for the advancement of life. The blind cannot lead the blind. In its deeper meaning, the "blind" are the people who have no sense of responsibility for life forms.

One cannot create leaders by voting for them because voting cannot cultivate or produce the sense of responsibility in those who win the votes. On the contrary, the winner's victory feeds his glamor, vanity, and pride and makes him feel that people are his possessions to be used the way he wants.

We see real leadership in the Indian Chief, Hiawatha. The first thing He demonstrated was His sense of responsibility by cleaning the lakes, rivers, and forests so that human beings could enjoy them. The second step He took was to create friendship, unity, and peace. The third step He took was to create an individual sense of responsibility toward oneself, toward others, and toward Nature and the Great Spirit. The fourth step He took was to speak about and demonstrate in His life total harmlessness and protection from one's own actions.[2]

It is a fact that one's own deeds come back and hit him. This is called the boomerang effect. The boomerang effect refers to the karmic consequences of our actions, words, and thoughts. Every expression is a flow or wave of energy which goes into space once it is released, carrying the motive of the originator. If the motive is evil, then the arrow of those words, actions, and thoughts is magnetically attracted to an evil target. If the target does not contain any evil, the aura of the target bounces the arrow quickly back to the source because of the evil contained in the source, and damages and contaminates the source, in the same way that one dumps garbage in a room and then is forced to stay in that room.

The speed of the return of the arrow is faster if more power is put into sending it to the target. Thus man condemns himself and pays the price for his evil deeds by his own hands.

The arrows are sent by different centers in the body —an etheric center, an astral center, or a mental center. When the arrow comes back, it usually hits a center which was put in action by an evil motive. This is how man becomes exposed to the arrows he sends toward his victims.

Leadership cannot stand strong, healthy, and prosperous if it does not stop the release of dark arrows. It is in its sending of dark arrows that the leadership exposes itself to self-destruction.

One can grow in strength, beauty, and wisdom if his arrows — namely his actions, words, and thoughts — carry benevolent thoughts to space. One may ask whether such benevolent arrows come back to their originating source. These arrows do not come back; but each time they are released from any center, they draw with them a flow of energy from the centers of will, love, and light, which then spreads into the aura of the sender and enriches it with harmony, health, strength, and bliss. This is why we are told that a good thought has a healing quality, and it also destroys some psychic germs which try to invade the aura.

Leadership, whether it is a person or a group, must remain harmless, not only toward others but also toward itself. Those who have inner guidance are extremely careful not to hurt other people or themselves and pollute space.

One of the most important duties of the leader is to dissipate glamor, illusion, maya, and the Dweller on the Threshold. These are psychological hindrances on the path of discipleship and initiation. Unless they are conquered and dissipated, no leader can be faithful to himself and others, and no person can step onto the path of leadership. Actually, the bottom line of all preparatory training for leadership is the eradication of these four obstacles.

To give a simple definition of these obstacles, we can say that when glamor and illusion control the etheric energy and condition the life of the person on the physical plane, making him follow the commands of glamors and illusions in his activities, sex life, eating, and drinking, then that person is in maya. He is living in an unreal, false world conditioned by his glamors and illusions. Maya is a state of crystallization in which the glamors and illusions take the form of concrete patterns in the etheric body.

We may also say that maya is that state of consciousness in which the human soul is identified with all physical, emotional, and mental forms which he created as a result of reactions and responses to life-events.

Glamor is an image of a desire, ambition, or dream which imposes itself on the astral field of force and blocks off the power of reasoning and logic. Glamor can be intensified very potently when it is combined with an illusion which it uses for its nourishment and support.

An illusion is always a thoughtform built around a pure idea, mixed with prejudices, superstition, misunderstanding, and selfish tendencies. For example, fanaticism is the activity of an illusion. When a person receives a pure idea but mixes it with half-truths and appropriates it to his own vanities and ego, he creates illusion. In every fanatic there is a pure idea, but he can neither see it nor make others grasp it because he dresses this idea up with half-truths, self-interest, pride, and blindness to the values of others.

The Dweller on the Threshold is the totality of maya, glamor, and illusion personified in man and identified with his personality.

The first major step of the leader is to make people learn detachment from their false images and not identify with their psychological states, moods, and urges. Leadership starts to create freedom from all those prisons which the human soul built and dwelt in through his ignorance.

It is true that many self-chosen leaders with no inner guidance lead people into disasters. How can people prevent the rise of a dictator unless democratic measures are taken against him?

The first fundamental step is to have a political or spiritual school which starts from age seven and continues to age forty-nine. In this school, seven basic principles will be taught during these forty-two years, with gradually increasing depth, intensity, and vision. The students will be carefully selected. These basic principles are

1. The development of the physical, emotional, and mental mechanism
2. The science of heroes
3. The unity of life
4. The operation of a supreme consciousness everywhere (taught through religion and legends)
5. The fundamental laws of Nature
    a. the Law of Synthesis
    b. the Law of Attraction
    c. the Law of Economy
    d. the Law of Karma
    e. the Law of Future or of Incarnation
    f. the Law of Building the Bridge
6. Sciences — astronomy, physics, chemistry
7. Politics and the future mankind

This school will educate the future politicians who will work for one humanity. From the beginning, the students must be educated to overcome all racial, national, religious, and sexual barriers and strive toward human consciousness. The spirit of separatism must be uprooted forever. They must be taught that they are human beings and that they will work only for the interest of one humanity.

Only those who show humaneness, selflessness, heroism, integrity, fearlessness, care for life-forms, tolerance, understanding, leadership qualities, simplicity, utter sincerity and frankness, silence, and detachment must be promoted and advanced. The others will be removed.

Leadership will come out of the ranks of these students.

During the last years of study, from ages forty-two to forty-nine, the students must go deep into the science of the Hierarchy and the study of the subjective world. From age seven to forty-nine, they must keep diaries of subjective experiences, such as dreams, visions, contacts, guidance, etc., which will be scientifically studied by Teachers.

After age forty-nine, the school, which is made up of students and various boards, will choose three candidates for leadership. One of them will be selected to be the supreme head by majority vote. The other two will act as his assistants and counselors and head the interior and exterior ministry. The school will provide the heads of all governmental branches from those who were trained in each specialization. The service period will last seven years, after which the leader can pass his position to someone else whom he may consider more adequate for the job. Possibly the Exterior Minister will take his place, moving the Interior Minister to the post of the Exterior Minister.

After seven years of service, the President will move on and work as a Teacher of graduate classes, enriching the students with his wisdom, knowledge, and experience. If the signs indicate that the President must continue another seven years, a one-year vacation must be given to him so that he can think about his agreement to stay as the Supreme Head. During this one-year period, one of his assistants will replace him. If his decision is not to stay, then the substitute will continue as the Supreme Head.

The school will have men and women. The women must be encouraged to be the heads of three departments:

   a. Educational

   b. Cultural

   c. Judicial

However, if they want, they can work in any department they choose.

This school will start as an international, world institution in which the best of all nations will be collected to be prepared to fill the posts vacant in their own country or anywhere else in the world. It will be better if, for example, an American becomes the leader of the Chinese, a Chinese student becomes the leader of France, and so on. When the students reach age forty-nine, they will already be specialized in their future field of service.

Once a year, all the leaders graduated from this school will hold a conference and report to their countries and the world what they did, what they could not do, what their plan is for the future, and why. The school will be open to all help that anyone can give, as long as no strings are tied to the help and the intention is to create a better future world community. Such a procedure will not give anyone the chance to be a dictator, to be totalitarian, or to use his field for separative or selfish ends.

If by any chance the supreme council of all graduated active leaders notices that one of the leaders is not behaving in line with the principles of the school, it will have the authority to take measures against him and send him back to the school for a lengthy overhaul.

The faculty of the school will be mostly women. They must be specialized in their fields, and after twenty-one years the faculty will be composed of students of the school.

Students can go to other universities for specialization, if the school does not yet provide the complete course for their interest. The main subject that will always receive special attention will be the science of the continuity of consciousness. This science will be arranged on such a gradient scale that the students will study it from the beginning to the end of their studies, practice it, and actualize it.

When we speak about inner guidance, we do not refer to mediums, channels, automatic writers, low psychics, or sensitives; but we refer to those who have the ability to function consciously on the physical, emotional, mental, and Intuitional Planes and according to their own experience conduct their leadership. Students of such a school must be able, by the end of their curriculum, to contact their Master of the First Ray Ashram and study the Plan of the Hierarchy in order to have a firsthand realization about his duties and responsibilities as a leader. His guidance must come through such contacts.

It is true that there are military and political schools in the world, but they are limited in their visions and service, and they serve special interests. The new school will be, literally, a human school for the benefit of all humanity.

Plato spoke about the philosophers leading the nations or humanity. Sages spoke about the externalization of the Hierarchy. These two concepts are the same. Humanity must be led by people who know what they are doing, who do not have the slightest sense of separatism, who are academically prepared and transformed to face their world service.

Certain leaders will argue about inner guidance, not knowing that most of the world leaders, from the dawn of history until now, have their consultants who are sometimes mediums, channels, astrologers, dreamers, men of God, or even superhuman beings. Even at the present, most of the leaders have private consultations with such people.

The new leadership will not depend on mediums, channels, psychics, dreamers, astrologers; but the leadership itself will build the continuity of consciousness to come in contact with the Hierarchy to receive guidance. Other methods are extremely dangerous and may lead a nation into a catastrophe.[3]

The new leadership will be trained in such a way that they can check each other or have consultations with each other about the direction or guidance the leader receives. It is the right time to start such a school. Twenty years later, it will be too late.

Notes:

1. See also *The Sense of Responsibility in Society*.
2. See *Hiawatha and the Great Peace*.
3. For information about mediums please refer to *Cosmos in Man, The Psyche and Psychism, The Other Worlds*, and *Breakthrough to Higher Psychism*.

18

Self-Confidence

One of the qualities of a leader is Self-confidence. Without Self-confidence, a leader cannot accumulate and transmit psychic energy, which is the factor that causes transformation and change of direction in others.[1]

Self-confidence can be cultivated gradually as one

1. Gains control over his personality vehicles

2. Fuses his consciousness with the consciousness of the Inner Watch

3. Does not waste energy

4. Does not do things mechanically

5. Does not do things against his own conscience

6. Does not act against the law of the unity of life

7. Does not increase the load of his karma through harmful thoughts, words, and deeds

8. Learns the seven basic laws of life and abides by them:

   — the law of Beauty

- the law of Goodness
- the law of Righteousness
- the law of Joy
- the law of Freedom
- the law of unity
- the law of synthesis

9. Expands his consciousness and develops insight and foresight
10. Develops the ability to see causes and motives behind events, actions, words, and ideas
11. Masters the subject of his interest or the topic about which he will talk or write or build his life around
12. Develops creativity
13. Becomes able to see the difference between artificiality and beingness, in himself and in others
14. Lives in the light of the Hierarchy
15. Destroys the seeds of vanity in himself
16. Keeps his nervous system and brain free from intoxication
17. Increases his psychic energy
18. Develops fearlessness, courage, and daring
19. Develops humility and solemnity
20. Develops enthusiasm
21. Learns to appreciate the value of others

Once Self-confidence is developed, the person is a powerful source of energy and guidance.

There are two kinds of self-confidence. One is written with a capital "S." The other is written with a small "s." Self-confidence with a capital "S" refers to a person who has liberated his consciousness from the lower vehicles and, to a certain degree, has succeeded in becoming his Self and found the treasures hidden in his being. Self-confidence with a small "s" is the result of an identification with wealth, position, or certain knowledge.

Professional people are mostly found in the second category, except those who, along with their academic knowledge, developed beingness. Wealth, position, and academic knowledge alone are slippery ground, and those who have a little insight do not feel too secure on it. But those who develop beingness stand firm in all conditions, even in all ages.

Alexander the Great met a man who lived in a barrel resting under the Sun. Alexander addressed the man, saying, "Why are you living such a life?"

Instead of answering his question, the wise man said, "Move away with your horse and do not obscure my sunshine."

The self-confidence gained by worldly power is always defeated by the Self-confidence gained by spiritual powers. This was demonstrated in the life of Moses, when prophet Nathan scolded King David, when Jesus rebuked worldly authorities, and in the lives of Socrates, Buddha, and all those who trod the same path. Self-confidence gained by spiritual attainment is power.

In olden days in ancient temples, when a person achieved true Self-confidence he was given a *staff*. The staff was the symbol of spiritual authority, the essence of Self-confidence, by which he used to lead his people toward light, love, and power. Every leader must have this spiritual staff — the Self-confidence to *evoke* beauty, joy, and light from those who come in contact with him.

Let us take the twenty steps to develop Self-confidence.

1. As long as one is controlled by his physical urges and drives, by his glamors, illusions, vanities, and ego he cannot achieve true Self-confidence.

2. The focus of his consciousness must move from the physical, emotional, and mental bodies into the higher mind and into the sphere of the Inner Watch. It is the Inner Watch Who gives the person the first "robe" of Self-confidence.

3. Waste of physical energy through a mechanical life, through slavery to urges and drives, through negative emotions, and through separative and uncontrolled thinking does not allow a person to achieve Self-confidence. Self-confidence needs energy to manifest, and every bit of energy helps to develop Self-confidence.

4. Every time a person does things mechanically or unconsciously, he creates factors in his being which act against his integrity. Without integrity and integration one cannot achieve Self-confidence.

5. Things done against one's own conscience create cleavages in his nature. Wherever cleavages exist, there cannot appear the power of Self-confidence.

6. Those who act against the Law of Unity defeat themselves in the long run. Self-defeat is the destruction of the structure of Self-confidence.

7. When one increases the load of his karma through wrong thoughts, words, and actions, his karma continuously creates disturbances and upheavals in his life. One cannot stand still upon the rolling waves. Self-confidence is stability and certainty.

8. The basic laws mentioned here are the source of psychic energy. Without these laws, man continuously hits his head against rocks. By living in harmony with these laws, he gains the power of Self-confidence.

9. Expansion of consciousness is not the result of academic knowledge or professional standards but the result of inner transformation. A theologian can write and speak about heavenly subjects but have a decaying consciousness. A physician can have the knowledge and skill to operate on hearts but be a heartless man. A scientist can create weapons of destruction but not be able to destroy his own habits. A financier can accumulate millions but be the slave of a cup of whiskey or sex.

Expansion of consciousness is the result of spiritual striving to realize the Plan behind life and the Purpose in life.

10. One who can see the causes of his thoughts, words, and actions can develop Self-confidence. But one who is subject to causes that control him is never able to develop Self-confidence.

11. A person who has Self-confidence, and inspires in others the spirit of Self-confidence, gains mastery over the subjects he wants to present to others. If he is building his life on an idea or an ideology, he must have in clear form all the knowledge possible about that idea or ideology. If he does not know and tries to impress people with his words, voice, or gestures, he not only confuses others but weakens himself and creates cleavages in his nature.

12. Creativity is a means to develop Self-confidence. One must prove to himself that he is somebody. Creativity is a process through which the Self manifests.

13. The person who wants to develop Self-confidence must train himself in the art of observing people. Such a person must try to see the difference between things that are artificial and things that are natural. Artificiality is a sign of weakness, spiritual poverty, insincerity, and hypocrisy. Self-confidence cannot be built upon such foundations.

14. It is only in living in the light of the Hierarchy that one receives continuous energy of Self-confidence. Without steady and increasing contact with the Hierarchy, one soon loses the source of his strength.

15. Vanity is a destructive element which creates cleavages in the person between his True Self and his personality. When the personality is separated from the powerhouse of the Self, the person can never achieve true Self-confidence.

16. One who wants to develop Self-confidence never ruins his nervous system and brain with alcohol, hallucinogenic drugs, sugar, and meat.

17. Psychic energy is increased when one does his best in all his service, labor, and study and records certain achievements. In every achievement a new supply of psychic energy is given to him. Sacrificial service is another source of psychic energy. Without psychic energy, one cannot develop Self-confidence.

18. Fearlessness, courage, and daring cannot be developed in one life. They need many lives to accumulate and fill the essence of man; but every day and in every life one must try to cultivate them because Self-confidence cannot exist without courage, fearlessness, and daring. These are the three powerhouses of Self-confidence in man.

19. Humility and solemnity are the robes of glory of a Self-confident person. Without these robes, self-confidence is repulsive and destructive.

20. Self-confidence is not inertia but enthusiasm, a fiery involvement with heart, mind, and spirit. Self-confidence is warm and full of radiating light and beauty. Enthusiasm is the charm of Self-confidence.

21. By appreciating the value of others, their beauty, and by developing admiration and joy for their attainments, you cultivate Self-confidence within yourself. The appreciation of greatness in others is a sign that you have Self-confidence. A person who has no Self-confidence is afraid to acknowledge the greatness of others because of his insecurity.

A leader must develop Self-confidence to be able to serve. To have Self-confidence means to live as a spiritual entity, as a Self. To have Self-confidence means to have the power to dissipate all thoughts, words, actions, and forms built upon artificial foundations. When Christ said, "You are the rock upon which My church will be built," He was referring to the rock of Self-confidence which is rooted in the awareness of one's own essential Divinity.

Self confidence slowly grows into Self-determination. Self-determination is the ability to tune in with Cosmic currents to fulfill the Cosmic Purpose in various levels, according to the states of consciousness of the levels.

People think that Self-determination is an imposition and success of various desires and personal aims or goals. Real Self-determination has nothing to do with personality goals, nothing to do even with national goals. It is a state of consciousness in which the human soul completely identifies himself with the labor of the All Self but carries out his part individually. His individual labor is a small part of the great labor but totally in harmony with it. We are told that no power can resist the progress of a Self-determined person because behind his labor stands the Cosmic Self, working through his individuality.

In Self-determination all that a person does is to manifest the One Self through all that he thinks, speaks, and does.

Self-determination cannot come into existence until a person demonstrates pure Self-confidence. Once a person advances to Self-determination, he realizes that Self-confidence was actually, in its essence, trust in the One Self.

Notes:

1. See also *The Mystery of Self-Image*, Ch. 10, "Self-Image and Leadership."

19

Toward Greatness

The greatest responsibility of a teacher or a spiritual leader is to challenge his co-workers and create heroes out of them. This concept must be emphasized and renewed in the consciousness of humanity.[1]

Each human being is originally motivated to be a Great One and a Greater One. This must be a vision in front of your eyes. And if you keep this vision long enough, eventually it will pull you toward greater and greater achievements.

People in all walks of life keep themselves busy learning, knowing, and using their knowledge to satisfy their pleasures. Such people miss the mark, miss the goal, and cannot bring into manifestation the original motive existing in their Essence. This motive is to manifest greatness, heroism, and glory. If this magnet, if this vision is not attracting and synchronizing your steps toward itself, you are becoming your own failure.

Life challenges you to transcend yourself. To transcend yourself does not mean only to learn, to know more, to do more, to accumulate and enjoy more. To transcend yourself means to create out of yourself a better human being who understands more, who sacrifices more, who renounces more, who manifests greater virtues and greater values.

You may accumulate physical objects, emotional pleasures, mental furniture, and data, but none of these helps in your unfoldment. You transcend yourself when your field of love is more inclusive; if you have additional senses to come in contact with higher realities; if you have more power over time, space, matter, and energy; if you can manifest more beauty, goodness, and light. This is the path on which you must walk toward greatness.

Your progress is guaranteed when you carry the concept of greatness in your mind and strive to actualize it.

Nature is created in such a way that it evokes greatness; it calls you the great "you." Nature challenges you, and eventually you begin to surpass yourself. Mountains with their snow peaks invite you to climb. As you climb, you feel first your human weaknesses; then you develop confidence in yourself. When you reach the summit you feel the spirit of victory and ecstasy. Your horizon is so wide and the scenery is so impressive. Later you see how transient you are in comparison to Nature, but this feeling is not a depressing one. It has a great joy in it, the joy of achievement and the joy of greater faith in yourself.

Waterfalls inspire you. They challenge you to utilize them, to use them, to be like them: ever-flowing, ever-giving, ever-creative. Oceans inspire you because they give you the sense of endlessness. If you try to swim and a huge wave takes you in its arms and rolls you and then throws you to the shore, you feel defeated; but such a defeat challenges you, and you create ways and means to conquer the ocean.

You see millions and millions of stars and a longing develops in you. What are they? Can you reach them? And you try to create ways to know them, to get closer to them. This is how Nature evokes greatness, beauty, and a sense of universality from you. Nature wants you to be great, wise, creative, because Nature is your mother.

The greatness perceived in Nature is the projected greatness existing in the Self within each human being.

Worship of beauty in Nature is a moment of fusion between the greatness in man and the greatness in Nature. And through the fusion of these two, man transcends himself.

When you meet Great Ones, They are revealed to you to the degree that you have revealed greatness within you. You understand the greatness of Great Ones to the degree of your own greatness. You understand Great Ones on the level where you are or according to what you are.

The whole existence is in the process of evoking greatness from you. Life is arranged in such a way that greatness is inevitable. People will continually surpass themselves and eventually will enter into superhuman evolution.

All failures and consequent pain and suffering are temporary. They exist in time and only for a while, and the unfolding human soul is aware of this. The time will come when the human soul will drop all his chains and step onto the path of his divine heritage. This path has two divisions: the path of natural evolution and the path of conscious evolution.

On the path of natural evolution the Spark in the mineral kingdom advances through the next kingdoms and eventually graduates into the human kingdom. This is a very slow process, and it is carried on by the forces of Nature outside of the Spark.

Conscious evolution starts the moment the human soul takes the first initiation and goes forward impelled by his own fire, by his own light, in cooperation with the fires of Nature and higher beings.

Advanced disciples, initiates, and Great Ones bring challenges and inspiration to "little ones" and lead them to a life of aspiration, dedication, and striving. When aspiration to greater values, dedication to higher beauties, and striving toward higher summits of achievement begin within a person, he enters into the path of greatness.

A hero is a Great One. A hero is a person who spiritualized himself, universalized himself, and reached a point of awareness where he is able now to evoke greatness in those whom he meets.

It is not easy to be a successful human being and reach high positions in society. It often requires a heroic spirit not to give up in front of all the obstacles which manifest themselves on the path. But to be a real hero is much more difficult because your obstacles and problems are not only outside ones, but they also manifest from your own nature and often chain your feet on the path of Self-actualization. When you are clear of inner obstacles, the outer obstacles help you as if they were vitamins.

One of the tasks of the Teacher is to remind you about your greatness, about how great you are in your Essence, and inspire you to bring out that greatness through all that you do. You must be great when you are shaking hands; you must be great when you are talking; you must be great when you are thinking and feeling; you must be great in your daily environment. You must be great in relation to yourself to such a degree that when you strip yourself of all vanities, pride, and show-offs, you will be convinced that your greatness remains as it is — unmoved and unshakable.

There is no greatness except when it is progressive. You are not great if you are no longer evolving or if your greatness is not providing the foundations for greater constructions.

Your progressiveness is your greatness, and your greatness must be remembered every moment you are in action. If you remember your greatness, you will develop a rare sense which is called an observing eye. This eye watches you while you think, feel, talk, and act. You can feel the presence of your Watching Eye.

After the development of such an eye, your life steadily runs toward greatness. In the mirror of the eye you see the things that should be eliminated from your life and the things that must be cultivated more to make you achieve greater heights. To live under the observation of such an eye is very uncomfortable for those who are not yet free from their personality identifications. But it is a great joy for those who strive and draw inspiration and courage from the ever-watching eye.

When this concept of greatness is established in your consciousness, it protects you from all kinds of attacks which try hard to make you believe that you are insignificant or a failure. This is what your environment generally does to you. This is often what your parents, sisters, brothers, husbands, and wives do to you. This is what the news-media and social powers do to you to such a degree that eventually you believe that man is a miserable, unfortunate, and failed creature on the surface of the earth.

Once you reach such a conclusion you act insanely and your real failure begins because, from that moment on, you consciously or unconsciously work to lower the standards of people — to depress them, control them, and use them for your own ends.

The duty of disciples is to save such people by manifesting greatness and helping them develop faith in themselves. *Man must have faith in his True Self. That is the foundation.* Such a faith can be restored in the hearts of people by those disciples or initiates who demonstrate acts of greatness, beauty, and goodness for them.

Christ said, "Do not be afraid of those who kill your body, but be careful of those who kill your soul." To kill a "soul" means to kill the faith that one has in himself, to kill the vision that one has for his future. When faith and vision are taken away, the "soul" is dead; and those who have dead souls can commit any kind of crime ever mentioned in our *book of crimes.*

When you face difficulties on your path of transformation, try not to say:

> I can't.
>
> It is beyond my power.
>
> It is difficult.
>
> It is impossible.

Who am I?

I don't believe I can do it.

These expressions make your success in the future more difficult. Instead, try to inspire yourself by the examples of those Great Ones Who never gave up and Who, because of Their difficulties, reached greater heights.

As the concept of greatness deepens in your consciousness, it destroys all those thoughtforms of failure imposed upon you age after age in many ways and leaves you free to achieve greater success.

Creative people are those people who were able eventually to overcome the network of thoughts of failure and face their own greatness. There is powerful opposition to this concept of greatness. Negative forces whisper in your ear, "What's the use of striving? All will end in the grave. Make money by all means. Enjoy your body, your stomach, and your sex; that is all you need. No one can be more than human *as if you were human.* Life is a great dream; enjoy every moment of it, even at the expense of others, because all that you can do is to enjoy life."

Such expressions form a web in your aura. This electrical web is built by words, emotions, and thoughts of failure; by words of discouragement and acts of jealousy, hatred, and injustice committed toward us. This web strikes us every time similar conditions are experienced.

A hero is a man who can make a breakthrough, liberate himself, and develop faith in the potentials hidden within him. This breakthrough is achieved by nourishing the concept of greatness.

There is another enemy against your concept of greatness. It is a very subtle enemy which destroys your striving toward greatness in such a subtle way that you do not feel it, and you even agree with it. This energy can be called the "belief that your outer success is your inner achievement." Physical, emotional, even mental success is considered outer success. Inner success starts with virtues, with the unfoldment of higher senses, with expansion of consciousness, and with communication with higher planes and higher centers. Inner success is measured by the extent of your sacrificial service and inspired creativity.

There is a very fine line between outer and inner success. Often outer success is achieved at the expense of inner success. Inner success is achieved by renouncing the results of outer success.

Because of the pressure of outer success, people live a life that is less than what they really can live in their essence, less than what they really know. They consider this a normal life. They identify themselves with the glamor of outer success, and they do not see the possibility of manifesting their spiritual achievements or living in the standards of their beingness and knowingness.

The glamor of outer success must be defeated through meditation and occasional observation. Meditation releases the inner potential, and observation helps the person to detach himself from the objects of his outer success.

Once the concept of greatness is rooted in your soul, nothing can stop your progress. Your faith in your own greatness becomes a fountain of joy and strength, a fountain of inspiration and creativity.

The road to real freedom starts with the faith that you develop in your innate greatness. You become free to the degree that you manifest your innate greatness. No one can be free and talk about freedom without being great.

Whoever keeps you as a slave of your inferiority complex is an agent of dark forces. He is the enemy of your progress, and you can defeat that enemy only by demonstrating your innate greatness, your beauty, your goodness, your compassion, your insight, your intuitive perception, and your creative fire.

You have yet another victory to achieve. This is the victory which you will achieve if you make yourself able to create inner greatness within your enemy. You must make him see your beauty, the greatness of your compassion, and your spiritual glory. This will be the greatest opportunity for him to make a breakthrough.

But if you defeat him, try to destroy him, try to humiliate him and make him lose his soul, he will be your trouble age after age and an obstacle on your path until you transform him.

You can never get rid of an enemy except when you transform him and create inner greatness in him. We tried to destroy our enemies age after age to get rid of them, but in fact we multiplied our enemies age after age; and everywhere we went, wherever we took incarnation, we met our enemies again and again in different races, with different skins, but with the same animosity and hatred. This is what the history of mankind shows.

Your enemy starts his fight by telling you that you are not worthy enough to live. Once you believe that, you will be defeated. In the next life you will use the same technique and take your revenge on your enemy. This will go on and on until one of you changes your technique of fighting.

It is to this change that Christ referred when He said, "Bless your enemies." In other words, work for their inner greatness, trying to reveal their beauty, goodness, and light. This is how you can conquer them and make your victory their success.

If a dark one wants to enslave you, he makes you believe that you are worthless. He creates those conditions in which you lose your faith in yourself. Immediately when you lose your faith in yourself, you surrender your body, your heart, and your mind to him and he uses you for his own ends.

You must not do the same thing to him if you do not want to be trapped by him later. You must work to make him great, to make him beautiful until he sees his essential Divinity. Once he sees his essential Divinity, he will be your co-worker to establish the Kingdom of God on earth.

The whole effort of Nature is to create glory, greatness, and beauty. You have the cooperation of all Nature in your striving toward greatness. When you give birth to your child, you want him to be greater than you are. This is a natural instinct, and the same is true with Nature. Nature wants her children to reach greatness. This is the whole purpose of Nature. This is what the book of Nature teaches. It says, "Live like these redwood giants. Be a Niagara Falls in your fiery creativity. Be as solemn as the majestic, snowy mountains."

Notes:

1. See also *The Ageless Wisdom*, Ch. 9, "Future Greatness."

20

Leadership and Miracles

People are attracted to miracles. Miracles attract crowds of people. People usually think that a miracle is a sign of affirmation of greatness or a spiritual achievement.

Many Great Ones performed miracles and led people into a greater understanding and into greater cooperation. But since the beginning of this century, Great Ones renounced all kinds of miracles. There are important reasons for this:

1. Miracles are not the signs of greatness or holiness. Evil forces can also perform miracles and deceive or mislead people.

2. A miracle creates disharmony in the universal network of energies. It is our imposition upon the Law of Karma.

3. Miracles develop vanity and pride, using the forces of admiration, worship, and devotion of people.

4. Miracles crystallize the consciousness of people in the image of the performer of the miracle.

5. They make man think in terms of phenomena, in terms of appearance and actions, instead of in terms of achievement and beingness.

6. They create jealousy, resentment, fear, and hatred. They develop inferiority complexes in people.

7. They force premature efforts to perform miracles. This creates a sense of failure.

8. Miracles develop expectations. People wait for miracles instead of seeing that man is the highest miracle in the Universe.

9. Miracles develop in people mechanical ways and means to utilize the secret knowledge for self-satisfaction and self-gratification.

10. Miracles usually impress the lower mind and create curiosity for personal interest. This interest is mostly related to physical health, emotional satisfaction, or to some revelations.

11. Miracles paralyze individual striving and effort to achieve a level of beingness in which man uses the laws and principles of Nature consciously and with efficiency.

12. Miracles increase the numbers of devotional beggars and eventually lead to great disappointments and denial.

A miracle is a forceful imposition of will upon energies and forces to materialize or dematerialize objects, to heal or kill a living being, or to reveal on the physical plane things that exist on higher planes. Such information is also an imposition upon the minds of people who are not yet ready to understand the mechanics behind the miracle.

It is possible by certain means to stop a plant's growth. In this act you disturb all the forces which are busy making the plant grow.

It is possible to materialize objects, by causing a malignant turmoil in the flow of the natural forces.

It is possible to heal through a forceful action and cause a great violation within the karmic network of the person.

It is possible to reveal supermundane facts to people, but disturb their consciousness for centuries.

The true miracle is the miracle of Self-actualization and cooperation with the laws of the Universe, without any violation.

Progress is not achieved by miracles. The human seed cannot grow and become an oak tree by sudden jumps. Achievement and progress are made through individual and collective labor, aspiration, and striving. Achievement is made through expanding one's consciousness and developing compassion. Achievement is made through manifesting virtues of the Soul and trying to live in the consciousness of one's Self.

Progress is a step-by-step achievement. A miracle is an act of stealing, violation, and trespassing.

There is a very sad statement in St. John's Gospel. It says, "Even though he [Jesus] had performed all of these miracles before them, yet they did not believe in him."[1]

Is it possible to believe that His crucifixion and suffering were the result of His miracles which did not serve the purpose for which He came? Did He come to make people believe in Him? I assume He was aware of it, and that is why He submitted himself humbly to the death on the cross. Another miracle to escape from the cross would have been a great violation of the law. His followers, being mostly miracle-addicts, created a whole legend of miracles.

Is this why humanity is on the verge of total self-destruction? Is this why we know so much, but we are so little?

Is it true that love leads us into superhuman efforts and sacrificial deeds, but the Karmic Lords are Watchful Eyes. This means that one can perform miracles to help people, but he will pay a heavy tax for his miracles.

In St. Luke we read, "When Herod saw Jesus, he was exceedingly glad, for he had wanted to see him for a long time, because he had heard many things concerning him, and he hoped to see some miracles by him."[2]

But He did not perform any miracle in front of Herod. He knew that the greatest miracle was He, Himself, standing in front of Herod. And He became a miracle, not by performing miracles, but by actualizing and manifesting the divinity in Him, through His Beauty, Goodness, Righteousness, Joy, and Freedom.

It seems to me that in His intense love for humanity He performed miracles, while being continuously aware that miracles would not build His true image in the consciousness of humanity but only His words, ideas, visions, and His ever shining beingness. He knew exactly what was awaiting Him because He knew the Cosmic Law in its detailed operation.

Can you imagine how hard and humiliating it was on the cross to hear the voices of the rulers saying, "He saved others; let him save himself, if he be the Christ."[3]

The methods that the Great Ones and Their disciples are using at the present are:

1. Telepathic messages broadcast toward disciples and Initiates to help them cooperate in greater detail with the Forces of Light.

2. The Science of Impression through which the Great Ones broadcast higher visions, ideas, and revelations to those who are ready to receive them and transform their lives. Impressions are broadcast to all, and those who are ready receive them and improve their lives.

Advanced ones use these impressions as the source of their creativity and enthusiasm, and they improve their physical, emotional, and mental health as far as their karma permits.

3. The third method which They use is inspiration. They inspire people and challenge them to advance on the path of perfection, and charge them to face greater responsibilities for world service.

Inspiration gradually releases the core of man and prepares him for greater receptivity of energies and currents coming from higher sources.

Their intention is to build the bridge between humanity, Hierarchy, and higher sources so that humanity (and through humanity, the lower kingdoms) can be guided on the road of perfection. In this way the laws of Nature are not used for personal ends and not violated to force changes in the consciousness of the people.

The greatest and most permanent successes cannot come through miracles. They come through readiness and transformation.

Spiritual progress cannot be achieved by consulting mediums and accepting their predictions related to your personality life, physical well-being, or financial condition. Spiritual progress is made when you yourself develop your own spiritual powers, contact with higher realms, and through receiving higher guidance improve your life and transform your entire being.

People think that their life is set like a machine, and it must work as a programmed machine does. This is not true.

You can change your future with your present thoughts, feelings, words, and actions. You can even overcome your karma with your striving and fusion with the power of Christ.

Man is destined to be the master of the Universe. Do not allow other people's opinions to decide for you. You decide for yourself.

Notes:

1. John 12:37
2. Luke 23:8
3. Luke 23:35

21

Leadership and Renunciation

Some mystics in the past emphasized renunciation from the world. They left all that they had and withdrew to mountains, caves, or deserts. There they impressed pilgrims with the idea that renunciation was the way to achieve spiritual values. Some of them achieved great heights on the spiritual path, not because they renounced their possessions and positions in the world but because through renunciation they set free their minds from worldly occupations and dedicated themselves to spiritual values.

Others remained in their positions and fought in the darkness to serve humanity and Hierarchy.

Renunciation also became an act of abandoning one's own duties, responsibilities, and karmic obligations. Thus, those who had more of a sense of spiritual values left the affairs of the world to those who had no interest in spiritual values. Thus the world was deprived, and materialism, greed, and selfishness grew in the absence of spiritually minded people.

True renunciation has nothing to do with leaving positions and possessions. True renunciation is not related to the objects of the world or to the positions in the world but to thoughts and vanities. One can have around him wealth and riches or one can be in a high position but still be a renounced person if he has detachment and is free from vanity.

When detachment is developed and vanity is dispersed, all that one has can be used for the service of others. Such a man can be an example for others in his responsibilities, duties, and karmic obligations.

A person who has renounced does not have images of properties in his aura. A person who is attached to his properties carries in his aura all the pictures or forms of the objects he owns. This is why one suffers mentally when he loses the objects he has. For a person who has renounced it makes no difference when the objects are taken away from him. A person who has renounced stands above his positions and possessions. Instead of becoming a source of vanity for him, they turn into an altar of sacrifice for the good of all. Because of his position, he brings greater Beauty, Goodness, Righteousness, Joy, and Freedom to the world.

Renunciation is a process of disintegration of glamors. Glamors are crystallized pictures of the objects of our desires. In renunciation we clear our aura of such objects and free ourselves from them. Glamors control us like machines and use our energies to satisfy their drives.

Renunciation is a process of clearing away our vanities. Vanities are formations in our mental body. They are images of ourselves built by our wishful thinking. A soldier thinks he is a king. This image is a vanity. The vanity interferes with his sense of reality and controls his thinking, words, and actions. He eventually develops confusion because reality and vanity fight within his nature, or the vanity does not prove to be true in his life and the reality cannot focus his attention on his duties.

Renunciation from vanities makes a man stable, realistic, straight, and productive.

Renunciation is like clearing our sky of clouds and letting the sunshine in.

Renunciation creates magnetism in our aura, and when a man is not attached to objects and vanities in his mind, the treasures of the Cosmos pour out in his direction. He accepts them but uses them to meet the needs of people around him.

The laws of Nature act very accurately. Those who renounce their glamors and vanities cooperate closely with the laws of Nature. What Nature gives to them they accept gratefully because they understand that whatever they have is whatever they gave to others. This is also true for our positions in the world. If we helped others and prepared them for higher and higher positions, they in their turn, by the laws of Nature, will help us to achieve greater positions, not for the sake of positions but for the sake of greater responsibilities and service.

Nature does not care about so-called positions. What is counted by Nature is our field of responsibility. True positions are the fields of our responsibility which we carry in honesty and gratitude and with a sense of humility.

Only the person who has renounced is the true person of his position, and only the person who has renounced can use his possessions in the right way. Glamors and vanities force us to use our possessions to increase our glamors, and they urge us to use our positions to increase our vanities and live in an unreal world.

Renunciation is a process of withdrawal into the greater light of reality and an act of creating a clear focus in our vision.

The leadership of spiritual groups must intelligently watch for glamors and vanities in the members. Those who have an increasing amount of glamor and vanity must be worked upon and cleared before new positions are given to them.

The downfall of spiritual groups starts when people full of glamors and vanities are promoted to higher positions and given higher responsibilities. Such people will only serve to increase their glamors, to multiply their vanities, and eventually create a chaotic condition in the group.

Glamors are dispersed by replacing them with virtues, and vanities are annihilated by replacing them with spiritual visions. Working on virtues eventually destroys glamors. Striving toward visions disperses vanities.

Leadership is not withdrawal from the world but a process of taking part in the struggle and striving of humanity.

It is also true that leadership is not a location but an interest and a responsibility. One can live in a cave but be active in the meetings of the United Nations, and one can be in the United Nations but live in a cave of selfhood and separatism.

22

Practical Suggestions

The leader needs people who will stand for the Teaching and for the group through which the Teaching is given.

Some members who have vanity about themselves and about their worth also have fear that damage may come to their reputation or interest. They cover themselves and do not stand for the Teaching and for the group. They like to hide, especially when they feel that the group or the Teaching is under attack. They hide to save their skin or self-interest.

Such people are very dangerous people, not only for the group but also to their own interests. At critical times they try to go to the side of those who attack the group or the Teaching, or they hide so that they are not involved in any conflict.

But it is interesting that the attackers know who belongs to the group. They pretend that they do not know about the person who hides himself so that they can use him against the group or isolate him through fear. When the attackers defeat the group, they turn to those who were hiding and expose them in hard ways.

If one wants to be a member of a group, he must commit himself to the service of the Teaching and to the service of the group. If he sees things he does not like, he has the privilege to complain officially or to resign. But nobility requires, once he sees a great value, that he stand for that value and become a witness.

We must never forget that we must be "a way by which men may achieve." We are not referring to showing off, babbling about the Teaching and the group; but we are referring to the honesty and sincerity of a member who feels joy and dignity to have the opportunity to be a member of a group which spreads a pure, honest, and constructive Teaching in the world.

There are also those who either have an inferiority complex or are not worthy enough to make people know that they are the members of the group or students of a lofty Teaching. This is a protection for the group, but instead of hiding themselves and keeping their own standards, they can strive and improve themselves and be proud of making themselves known as members of the group.

The leadership of the group must be very careful of both these types of people because they can create suspicion and make intelligent people feel that there are things in the group which are hidden or dangerous.

A true member of the Teaching must stand as a witness for the Teaching. He must suffer and even be persecuted for the Teaching. This is how the Teaching is spread and the Plan of the Great Ones is fulfilled.

"Of all the depraved traits of humanity one must subtly note faintheartedness. This quality borders on many other dark traits. Nearest of all is treachery. Faintheartedness borders on fear, cowardice, and selfhood. And in the Fiery World there is no place for faintheartedness. And the crown of courage can be placed only on the brow which is bared in self-renunciation. Yes, let the lone warrior fight single-handed. Let the arrows of hypocrites pierce his breast. Let each manifest aspiration be met with rejection. Yet will his armor be studded with courage . . . . Faint-heartedness is slavery of the spirit. Only the head which bows not in faintheartedness will be adorned with the great crown . . . . Verily, faintheartedness and self-deception are sisters of darkness!"[1]

In the Teaching we are told about trust. This is such an important word. The leader must teach his co-workers how to act trustworthily, how to be trustworthy. For example, if a co-worker is put in charge of a group or a store for books or other articles, he is entrusted with certain duties:

1. His first duty is to make a very thorough inventory of all that is handed to him for the group work.

2. He will check his inventory at regular intervals and add or remove certain items. He will add items as they are received; he will remove items that are old or destroyed.

3. If he sends anything, he will send it with a voucher which contains a detailed explanation of what was sent. When he receives things, he will add them to the inventory and acknowledge to the leadership exactly what he received.

4. When the period of his service is over, his responsibility is to hand over to the next worker exactly what he has in the inventory and be ready to give the reason (and proof) for things removed from the list.

There are many instances when people donate certain things to the group, but part of these things do not reach the group. Directly or indirectly they are assimilated. The duty of the man in charge is to take all that is given to him and deliver to the group exactly what he received, even with the signature of the giver.

If any item is given to another group, the duty of the man in charge is to know where it is and how it was delivered. Nothing should "disappear."

It is very important to emphasize the point that the person in charge is responsible for all that was handed to him. This is how law and order are kept alive and much confusion, ill feelings, and loss are prevented in a group.

Irresponsibility in a group is like a gopher that eats the roots of a growing group and brings disaster upon it.

Money is a very important factor. All that comes in and goes out must be registered in detail, and the man in charge must be ready every moment for an audit.

There is another practice in certain groups regarding donated articles. Some members ask for certain donations (mostly articles) from people and choose for themselves those things which they like. This is a very ugly practice, and the leader must be careful that such activities are not practiced in the group.

The leader must cultivate utmost trustworthiness and honesty within co-workers, and dishonesty in word or behavior must be considered a severe danger for the group.

No one can walk on the path of perfection without honesty and trustworthiness.

The Board of Directors is the custodian of all that the group has. It is important that every time the members of the Board change, the former ones officially hand over to the new Board whatever they had in their inventory. Without this practice many headaches and problems may arise.

It is possible to have confusion and conflict within the leadership group. To handle this situation without any damage the leader must take the following steps:

1. Have a meeting as soon as possible to observe the situation clearly.

2. See if it is a personality conflict or a difference in understanding or vanity or jealousy.

3. See clearly the origin of the conflict and the possible effect of it.

4. Allow the conflicting parties to express their ideas and feelings as openly as possible.

The meeting must be held under strict principles:
    a. Only respectful expressions must be used.

    b. Efforts must be made to see the viewpoints of others.

    c. Personality interests must be renounced.

    d. Mistakes must be admitted.

    e. Joy must be expressed.

    f. There must be thought about the welfare and the future of the whole group.

    g. There must be the spirit of gratitude.

The leader must emphasize these seven principles under which the discussion must be held.

The leader must condemn no one and hold no side.

The discussion can continue for weeks or days, but between intervals the leadership group must promise to keep all discussion within the leadership group and not involve the membership.

After each session the leader must reserve five to ten minutes to give a future vision to the leadership group and try to make them subordinate their feelings and thoughts to the greater vision of the future.

It is a good idea to have a dinner with the leadership group after each meeting and during the dinner not discuss any problem whatsoever.

At the end of the meeting or series of meetings the leader must ask for a vote of confidence and make his decision or judgment which will be final. Before the vote of confidence the parties must agree to hold the leader's judgment final.

After the decision or judgment the leader must hold a firm position, and the group members must respect his judgment with honesty and nobility.

Every weakening of the core attracts attacks from dark forces. Every time the core passes through a crisis and overcomes the difficulties, the creative forces rejoice and inspire the core for greater activity.

After problems are settled, no names or past stories must be mentioned any more.

Sometimes people call for help asking the group to pray or meditate for them for certain problems of health or other difficulties. The one who is contacted for help must NOT describe the sickness to the group members but only say, "This fellow needs help and we must pray."

We do not want images of sickness or complications to be impressed upon the minds of the group members. It *can* open a channel of attack by exciting the imagination.

The leader must be careful not to contaminate the imagination of the group with a detailed presentation of the problem. Such actions bring fear, tension, depression, and negative imagination into the atmosphere of the group.

The leader will deal with such demands with indifference, coolness, and the knowledge that all that happens, happens for the good and that karma knows what is going on.

Of course, the group can help, but not against the karma and not for any personal interest. The group help will be to destroy any attack upon the person.

Do not agitate the minds and hearts of the group by spreading the descriptions of troubles. Remember that all thoughtforms have effects, and certain people can take your news as posthypnotic suggestions. Great damage can be done with the intention to help someone.

Applicants for leadership must be trained in such a way that

1. They love labor.

2. They do not reject any new task presented to them.

These two factors are considered two conditions for candidates' admittance to leadership. They must feel intuitively and accept consciously that their lives will be composed of endless labor. The labor will be carried on in spite of conditions, with joy and enthusiasm. It is good to remind the candidates of these factors at the beginning of their training.

The candidates must be watched carefully at the time of labor. There are three kinds of candidates:

   1. There are those who work but complain and have resistance in themselves to labor.

   2. There are those who work mechanically and try to finish to have a rest.

   3. There are those who feel increasing joy, work with enthusiasm, and expect more labor.

Those who complain rarely pass the tests of leadership because they expect rewards, want recognition, or are anxious to jump into the hot pool of their pleasures.

Those who work mechanically do not grow spiritually through labor. Their consciousness remains the same. There is no striving in them. Their hearts are asleep.

Those who feel increasing joy in labor overcome their weaknesses and climb the ladder of leadership.

Watch how people work, and teach them to keep a diary of their reactions during their labor. If the diary is kept correctly, it will reflect the condition of their hearts.

The second test for the candidates of leadership is more difficult. During their labor, before they have finished it, new tasks are presented to them. Here again one must watch the reaction or response. Some of them think,

   "O, my Lord, another task?"
   "I can't do it."

"What am I gaining?"
"I am already tired."
"Well, let me do that also."

And negative thoughts and negative emotions begin to cloud their face.

Some of them accept the new task but put it aside and forget about it, until they feel they have the time and are in the mood to do it.

There are also those who reject it.

Few are those who feel great joy and accept the new task as if it were a great gift for them. They not only accept it joyfully and enthusiastically but also immediately see how to do it in order to receive new tasks for the future. They do not count the hours or the days because they feel that the path of leadership is incessant labor. They also understand that true labor does not exist if it is not done in joy and in enthusiasm.

Some children manifest such attitudes. They love labor and they ask for it. They are the ones who must be taken into the sphere of your heart, and opportunity must be given to them especially for leadership training.

Leadership training does not end in one life or in many lives. Once it starts it continues forever because it is the training to accept responsibilities on gradually higher planes, in greater areas of labor. And if one wants to know where the chains of responsibilities will end, he must remember Infinity!

But the true candidate for leadership takes a deep breath in joy because he feels gratitude for the limitlessness of Infinity and for the endlessness of labor and responsibility.

During the training of candidates one also meets those who seemingly work joyfully and enthusiastically but with wrong motives. They want positions from which to rule and to take over the groups for separative interests. They know instinctively that they cannot gain leadership positions if they do not demonstrate labor and acceptance of new tasks.

The leader can unveil their motives by suspending them from their labors and ignoring them for a period of time. In such a test those who have wrong motives will feel very uneasy, rebellious, gossipy, touchy, irritable, and will find or create opportunities to try to hurt the leader. They will show signs of impatience. They will even feel despair because they cannot reach their goals. Time is very important for them.

Another test for such people is to give them tasks that they hate or tasks that have no relation to the field of endeavor of the group. The leader may also engage them in organizations that are full of clever but selfish leaders. Through these tests the true colors of candidates eventually appear.

During such tests a born leader feels indifferent and passes the tests with a peaceful heart.

Forceful attachment to the labor and to the task is often the result of wrong motives and a personality drive.

Of course, one can copy the answers of the tests and often pass the exams, but on the freeways of life there are many who watch your speed and the way you drive and reach special conclusions.

Some people show cooperation in taking lots of responsibilities on their shoulders, not with the intention of helping you but to gain power over you and make their increasing demands be put into action. They think that the leader will collapse if they withdraw all their commitments of responsibilities.

The leader must be very careful not to depend on the work of one person. Instead he should give duties to several people so that he does not fall under the control of those who come to help him with doubtful motives.

A true leader-to-be rejoices when his leader presents more difficult tests for growth and challenges him to overcome more personality characteristics unworthy for the service. When a leader prepares a candidate for leadership he must find ways and means to bring out those lines of character which need to be eliminated on the path. When the candidate for leadership shows signs of resistance to growth and expansion, it means he is having difficulty overcoming elements which are not worthy to be carried by him.

If a piece of raw iron wants to be a useful instrument for service, it allows itself to be put into the furnace of discipline and, further, it allows itself to lie on the anvil and be beaten. The hammering of the iron is needed for its own transformation. It is impossible to bypass the furnace and the hammers if one wants to transform his life and make himself ready for leadership.

Joy remains again the greatest sign when one is under the hammer.

Those who carry the seeds of betrayal in their hearts rebel against every disciplinary move of the leader. This rebellion is a sign of a great danger in the future. The leader's duty is to find such seeds and expose them for removal or burning. The removal and burning of the seeds cannot take place except through the cooperation of the candidate for leadership. It is joyful acceptance of the hammering that brings the needed change in consciousness.

Fear is another sign that there are hidden factors in the candidate which in the future may endanger the work.

A true candidate for leadership does not worry that he could be temporarily removed from his duties because he has faith in the laws of Nature and faith in the leader.

Fear is the worst advisor, and very often it is fear that leads the candidate into apparently fearless actions and expressions. Fear prepares those traps in which the feet of the candidate are caught and his future usefulness is delayed for years or lives.

Another habit which must be hammered by the leader is the vanity of the candidate. When the candidate begins to show off and judge his fellow candidates as being inferior to him, he is in danger of losing his path. The leader must not lose time in warning him.

A vain person is like a person who has no sense of shame. One must be stern toward vanity.

The leader-to-be feels in his heart that he must prepare himself for the coming storms and darkness, and he is not concerned about his personal feelings during the discipline. One can easily overcome an army of stupid emotions and feelings at the moment of confrontation with a great crisis. Crises and calamities have a special fire which also burns away our vanities. And a leader prepares himself to face chaos and darkness.

The salvation of humanity is in the hands of true Leaders.

Notes:

1. Agni Yoga Society, *Fiery World*, Vol. III, para. 217.

23

Leadership and the Mystery of Manifestation

The new leadership will stay away, as much as possible, from crystallized dogmas and clichéd formulas. But the leader will be very careful not to build new dogmas and doctrines from what he believes.

People understand things according to their level. In each level, they create forms and ladders to climb. Thus, every explanation of great issues of manifestation is valid as far as the level of the people dealing with it is concerned.

The new leadership does not force its new understanding on others but tries to expand their consciousness to such a degree that they begin to look for new explanations. None of our explanations of the great issues of Creation can be final because human consciousness is not yet ready to understand entirely the issues related to Cosmic manifestations.

The greatest help one can offer to himself and others is to look at issues from ever wider perspectives and be open for new explanations and revelations.

In regard to how this manifestation came into being, the Teaching at the present offers the following explanations:

In presenting the Absolute, we make the mistake of talking about gods who are yet imperfect. Whatever their level, they are far away from the Absolute.

We think that all these globes, systems, and galaxies are created by the Absolute. This is what the common understanding is. The fact is that every progressive life-form, from the atom to the most complicated galaxy, is created by the evolving life-unit. This is what evolution is. The Absolute created nothing. He (if we can use such a word) radiated Himself as the Central Absolute Sun. His Rays went out in seven Cosmic gradations into Space and turned into atoms. By the Magnetic Law of the Central Absolute Sun, the atoms began to search for their home and find the path, their Ray.

It is these returning atoms in their many variations, from the atom to Galactic Logoi, which are creating all that exists on all planes. Each atom is trying to reach the Absolute by creating ladders, forms to advance further. Ladders or forms are built from the substance of the plane on which they are active. The are built for Self-discovery or as reflectors of their stage of beingness.

Bodies, vehicles, ladders, and mirrors[1] are also manifestations of the stage of the life-unit on the path to the Infinite. Matter, from which these forms are built, is what they were in the past while returning home. Every time the ray advances, it leaves behind a condensed energy —matter — which reflects what it was in the past. Other life-units use this residue to build other forms.

A blooming flower is an advancing ray or a life-unit. It becomes aware of its progress only through blooming and then surpassing that state and entering another form of expression.

Each life-unit or ray makes mistakes, no matter where it is on the path, as long as it is not yet reunited with the Absolute. These mistakes come into being through identification with the form it created.

Manifestation began by a motion or action. Karma is perpetual motion or action, as far as the manifested Seven Cosmic Planes are concerned. Any perpetual activity causes things to be, to change, to be transformed, or to be transmuted. It perpetually "creates" causes and cause-effects. This is why the Cause of all that is is motion, action. Action is karma, and it will not be a mistake if we call karma the "first cause."

We think that karma is the accumulation of our actions or our debts which we must pay. Such an understanding is limited. Karma is *action*. It is karma that creates, sustains, destroys, and rearranges things according to the programming put into actions in the mechanical and semiconscious states.

Everything is mechanical until the action becomes conscious, superconscious, and Cosmic conscious. The emanations, being from the Essence of the Causeless Cause, are in the rays and in the crystallized atoms. Each of them has its freedom to act. It is in freedom that the whole variety of things comes into being.

There are many kinds of actions. Initial Cosmic action is a pure emanation or radiation from the Source of the All-Conscious. Interactions of the emanations are on various levels:

1. Mechanical
2. Selfish
3. Group-interested
4. Semiconscious
5. Conscious
6. Superconscious
7. Cosmic conscious

When actions pass into the level of conscious action, the unit of beingness begins to undo things he did, or to introduce actions contrary to his previous actions. Then gradually he harmonizes his actions to the programmed purpose of the Primordial action. It is through this harmonization that eventually his consciousness enters into the stage of superconsciousness and fuses with the Cosmic Consciousness, as a Cosmic Consciousness.

When speaking about imperfect gods, we can refer to atoms, all life-forms, vegetables, animals, humans, angels, Great Ones, the Planetary Life, the Logos, the Solar Logos, the Galactic Logos. All these lives are relatively imperfect, but they are on the way to perfection. Every system has its own boss, and these bosses are not always in agreement with each other's goals or laws.

We as humans are subject to the Solar Laws, and we have to obey the laws the Solar Logos formulates. If we want to submit ourselves to other laws, we must raise our consciousness to a higher plane than the plane where the Solar Logos functions.

In Cosmic Space, the Great Lives are in the process of experimentation, integration, and alignment; but they are not yet in total alignment or harmony. As they enter into greater harmony with the advanced Life-forms, all their cells and atoms and kingdoms will be included in greater harmony with each other.

One can begin to serve this harmonizing process when he enters into a conscious state of beingness.

Karma controls all actions on all planes. It is the perpetual motion within all forms on all planes — action and reaction, cause and effect, flow as a perpetual motion. Winding and unwinding goes on all the time, until one reaches the conscious level where he starts to program himself differently and relate himself to conscious types of life-units.

Man in his essence must realize that he is a part of the Causeless Cause, caught up in the ebb and flow of karma; and he must find a way to work for his own salvation.

One may ask, will this manifestation continue forever as it is, coming into existence cyclically and disappearing, and repeating again and again; or will the human life continue as it is, with wars, revolutions, disturbances, diseases, famines, depressions, pleasures, successes, failures? The answer is very simple. As long as we do not act on the conscious or super-conscious level, as long as we do not change action, these things will perpetuate themselves in various forms but be the same essence.

This is why every human being must try to know what he is. He must try to know why things are going the way they are, why he is doing what he is doing, what is his goal. This will slowly lead him to understand the Law of Karma. When the Law of Karma is understood, the life of the planet will change.

The Great Lives of the Angelic and Divine Hierarchies were not created as such. Throughout billions of ages the members of such Hierarchies progressed from the human stage and eventually reached their present level. They are all trying to be co-workers to that unknown Cause, the evidence of which is the Law of Karma.

It is clear that the first Cause, or the Causeless Cause, did not create. It radiated. It spread Itself. The creators are those who developed light, love, will, and consciousness. The Solar Logos created our solar system; the Planetary Logos created the Planetary Life. Their creations are their own and are in harmony with Higher Beings, in which they serve as organs.

There is a great difference between radiation, manifestation, and creation. In creation, you use what is external to you, applying your mind, your will, etc. In radiation or manifestation, there is nothing outside that is used, but you radiate what you are. You exist in your own radiation. You are present in every atom you radiate. This is why the Absolute is everywhere, in everything. In reality, It is everything manifested.

From this viewpoint, you can see how the Absolute is present in every atom, in every living form, flower, tree, animal, and man. They have their relation with the Absolute in the degree that they are conscious of the Absolute within themselves.

With such a concept, you feel that you are living in your Home and every living form is not a stranger but presents a part of your essence. And you realize that the way you live either helps them to progress or retards their progress, which in essence is your own progress.

Notes:

1. Mirrors are built by Intuitional substance to watch our self image that we created and to see ourselves and our progress objectively on many dimensions. No one can advance without periodically looking into the mirrors of his self image. After one crosses the threshold of the Third Initiation, mirrors not only reflect our image but also the image of our co-workers.

24

Ever-Moving Forward

Orderliness is emphasized in the Teaching as the best way to progress, to achieve, and to save energy and time. But the orderliness which builds organizations and machines can also become the most hideous enemy of the progress of the spirit. One must be on guard not to make his orderliness and organization his own grave and bury himself in it.

An organized life must be ever-progressive. It must renew itself under the power of the person's expanding consciousness. Each expansion of consciousness must break a former level of orderliness and raise it to a new level, to serve as a gear for higher wheels.

The progress of life is hindered more by crystallized orderliness than by disorderliness. When one's orderliness becomes concrete, it creates dogmas, doctrines, traditions, impositions, and eventually totalitarianism.

Orderliness must be an ever-inclusive process, spirally achieving greater and greater heights. Anything organized turns into an obstacle on the path of progressive forces, which wastes time and energy to overcome it.

An organization must turn into an organism — a living, growing, and expanding entity which is capable of fitting new conditions and reaching new heights without losing its orderliness.

One must watch disorderliness and orderliness with the same attention. An orderliness which turns into a habit must be broken, and a new rhythm must be established. This is equally true in the physical, emotional, and mental natures.

Wrongly oriented political powers cannot exploit and misuse unorganized masses, so they try to organize groups, churches, and parties in order to be able to control them and use them for their own interests. It is easy to infiltrate organizations and run the machine, but it is almost impossible to rule an unorganized crowd.

Highly orderly and organized races or civilizations are closer to destruction than those which are less organized. This is because of their inability to surpass their crystallizations. This is also why, in Lemurian and Atlantean times, the survivors were those who were not in organized spheres but were living a primitive life. A similar thing will happen at this time if atomic and space war starts; the first target will be the most organized center.

Thus, a highly organized civilization is not a guarantee of survival. Such a civilization can only survive if in the right time it sees its crystallizations and barriers and bypasses them or transcends them.

An organization must turn into an organism so that it continuously heals itself of any hindrances, limitations, or sicknesses which are preventing it from growing and surpassing itself.

As in the Universe, so in man. New expansions of consciousness follow each other at a rhythmic pace. Each expansion of consciousness creates a pressure upon the organized life and presents a new challenge to strive for a higher level of organization. If the organization of physical, emotional, and mental habits resents it, then the conflict starts and the organization breaks; the habits break; the emotional and mental ways of life break; the dogmas, doctrines, and beliefs break, sometimes very painfully.

But if the organization responds to the expansion of consciousness or to the release of new energies, the life latent in the organization progresses, advances, and builds a new order, a new organization to meet the needs of the expanding consciousness or to meet the challenge of new energies.

Life is progressive, and eventually it destroys all that hinders it progress. To run in harmony with the progress of life, one must make shoes but immediately stop using them and make new ones when his feet grow.

People think that a growing consciousness cannot operate without sophisticated machinery. This is not true. A consciousness that is growing in the right direction needs less machinery, less rules, less laws, and more simplicity. As long as a consciousness depends on machinery, in the end it becomes the slave of the machinery.

Also, an expanding consciousness does not need an organized religion or political ideology but freedom from them. Freedom means the ability to go beyond one's mental fabrications.

Order and organization in the Cosmos is the foundation upon which all rests; but this order or organization is not one-dimensional, flat, or horizontal but spiral. Actually, two spirals are intersecting each other: one is rising and one is descending, continuously eliminating any crystallization in progressive transformation.

Orderliness in the Cosmos is not static but ever-progressive. Otherwise, how would the process toward perfection be sustained? The spirit in man traveled through many kingdoms. In each kingdom he organized his life and followed certain patterns. But his emancipation began the day when his organized life no longer fit his expanding consciousness, and he began to disengage himself from his organized life and try to build a more appropriate life which is able to function more freely.

Thus unless one can free himself from the set limits of a former level of life, he cannot start building a life which will translate a growing consciousness and a rising aspiration.

There is a very serious mental sickness which can be called "contraction." This word must be explained in order to be clearly understood.

Contraction is a mental phenomenon in which the consciousness loses its interest in essentials and focuses itself strongly on dead letters and on transient things with which the person identifies. Fanaticism is one of the manifestations of such a disease.

Another of its manifestations is concentration on a small part of an object and overlooking the importance of the purpose of the whole. Such diseases are very contagious and almost control our life everywhere in the world.

Contraction causes the formation of tumors on the body which use the energy of that body against its own survival. The pursuit of separate and selfish interests is a contraction. Seeing things from one viewpoint leads to contraction. Every kind of activity which has no interest in the welfare of one humanity, of one global life is contraction.

In my childhood I had a friend who, whenever he would see a good horse or an orchard, used to say, "That is my horse. That is my garden." One day I said to him, "That horse has an owner. That orchard belongs to Mr. So and So."

"Well," he said, "if the horse is not mine, it does not exist. If the orchard is not mine, no one owns it."

Such a psychology in different disguises, exists in the hearts of many adults and many leaders. If something does not belong to them, there are three possibilities:

a. It must be owned by them by any means.

b. It must be destroyed.

c. It must be assumed that it does not exist.

This is the same sickness of contraction in which the person identifies himself with objects and forgets the rights of others. From the same sickness originate the acts of fabrication, distortion, cleavages, conflicts, and wars. This sickness can only be cured when the patient is helped to see the interests of all; to see the forest and not the trees; to see the synthesis not the parts; to see the purpose or the summit and not the paths.

Orderliness in the Universe is a progressive movement to synthesize and a continuous effort to make a whole. Organizations and orderliness which do not harmonize their steps with the process toward synthesis are outworn, obsolete remnants of the past which act as hindrances on the path of evolution.

Any crystallization on mental, emotional, or physical levels is contraction. Organized systems of thought, organized and crystallized ways of feeling, organized ways of acting or habits are all contractions.

The human being is not a form in essence but a flow, a wave in the ocean of Cosmic energies. He is a flow that must always run in harmony with the rhythm of the Great Ocean. Any crystallization in his nature or restriction of his freedom is crystallization or contraction. Any contraction or crystallization is crushed by the other waves with intense suffering and pain in order to restore the flow which is rhythmic and progressively orderly.

One must organize his life and its activities for a closer and greater attunement with the expanding consciousness of man, of the planet, and beyond. This organization and orderliness can be pictured in the movements of a dancer who is trying to synchronize her movements to the ever-changing rhythm of the music and to the increasing speed of the music, and also trying to translate through her movements the ever-deepening meaning and significance of the music.

I knew a mathematician who was asked one day to prepare a schedule for the arrivals and departures of the buses in a city. He prepared one. A year later, he changed it to adapt it to the schedule of the trains. A few years later, he changed it again to adapt it to the schedule of ships and airplanes in the city. Eventually he organized a master schedule that related buses, trains, ships, and airplanes.

The same must be true for your physical, emotional, mental, and spiritual realms. All schedules must be continuously changed to fit each other and to maintain the smooth flow of the energy of relationship. But the story does not end with man. If one wants further progress, he must adapt his schedule to the schedules of higher and higher worlds.

Crystallization of organizations is not the only danger and hindrance to progress. There is another danger which creates more chaos than crystallization. When an organization falls into the hands of those who have special interests based upon their hatreds, greed, and jealousy, the organization slowly turns into a political weapon against those who have similar interests and also against those who oppose their self-interests.

This can be seen all over the world. When an organized entity, like a big elephant, falls under the rule of a monkey, people blame the scientific mind which produced the modern technology, pollution, and the danger of annihilation. But when we look more closely at the problem, it will be clear that the mind created all these as a response to certain human emotions — namely, hatred, greed, and jealousy.

These three enemies of mankind misused the mental powers and knowledge of man and directed them toward destructive ends, toward activities which do not guarantee the survival of the human race. The increase of knowledge is the most dangerous weapon against our survival if it is controlled by hatred, greed, and jealousy. These three vipers originate and are controlled by the astral plane, and it is very difficult to wipe them out. This is why more advanced knowledge will not be given to humanity until humanity is able to surpass hatred, greed, and jealousy.

Emotions control life. Imagination controls reason. Knowing these things, the ancient Adepts did not pass any knowledge to the neophyte until they believed that he was cleared of these three vipers.

Hatred is the flame of self-interest. Greed is the flame of self-interest. Jealousy is the flame of self-interest. These three flames are the destructive astral flames which overrule man and use his knowledge for his own self-destruction.

25

Forgiveness

Forgiveness is one of the esoteric and most outstanding characteristics of a disciple. When a disciple is non-forgiving, he is always reminding himself of or remembering things that occurred in the past. He is attached to the past and cannot progress, becoming instead a hindrance on his own path.

A disciple is known by his quality of forgiveness. On the path of initiation, forgiveness must increase and become universal. There are people who cannot even forgive little things that happen in their personality and group relations. But once a person starts to grow and become a traveler on the path, his forgiveness expands daily.

Christ gave the lesson of forgiveness to a man who asked whether he should forgive his brother seven times. Christ said, "You are not going to forgive seven times, but seventy times seven, and more." Then He gave a beautiful parable about a rich man who had lots of servants. One of the servants owed the rich man one thousand dollars and could not pay it back. The servant went to the rich man and said, "Master, I am not able to pay you this money. Can you forgive me for it?"

The rich man looked at him and said, "It is forgiven."

The servant was very happy and started for home. On the way he met a friend who owed him one dollar. He grabbed his shoulders and said, "You owe me one dollar, and if you do not pay it I am going to beat you. I want it now." And he started to beat the man.

At that moment, the rich man was passing by and saw what was happening. He became angry and said, "You bad servant, I forgave you for one thousand dollars, and you can't forgive one dollar? You know he doesn't have it. Because you acted very foolishly and unkindly, you are going to go to prison until you pay back the last cent of that thousand dollars."

After Christ told this story, He added, "Those who forgive will be forgiven."

What does forgiveness do for us in our lives?

1. Forgiveness releases us from painful thoughtforms. Whenever something painful happens, it makes us suffer. For example, if someone took our jacket and did not return it, if someone said naughty words to us or did something bad we did not like, these things are registered as painful events in our aura. All of us remember such events. Painful events can be registered in either the mental, emotional, or physical body. Once we forgive things and let them go, we release these thoughtforms and they start to disintegrate.

A thoughtform can act as an ulcer in our mental or emotional body. These ulcers, formed by painful thoughtforms or emotions, eat the aura and cause irritation. Such disturbances eventually enter the glands and cause many physical problems. The roots of these disturbances are nonphysical, and they are not easily found.

I suggest that every day at sunset we spend five or six minutes forgiving those against whom we have had bad feelings. Christ said, "Let not the sun set upon your anger." This is a psychological key for better health. Anger is a thoughtform of non-forgiveness. Just before the sun sets, try to forgive; get rid of your anger and throw it out. If you go to sleep with a thoughtform of anger in your mind, you will take it from your brain and pass it into your emotional and mental bodies when you sleep. When you withdraw from your body during sleep, you work in your emotional or mental body. The germs of anger will be more effective there, and they will actually eat your subtle bodies. Non-forgiveness also creates a magnetic rapport between you and the painful and unforgiving thoughtforms of others in space. Thus you increase the pollution of space.

2. Non-forgiveness causes tension and irritation in our nervous system and creates imperil. Imperil is a poison accumulated in the nervous system. Irritation burns the etheric body and creates a sediment called imperil which settles on the nadis, or etheric nerves. Wherever this sediment settles, the nervous system becomes numb. When this occurs, you cannot carry the electricity of psychic energy, or life-energy, to the physical body and the glandular system.

When you are unforgiving, you are always reminding yourself of the hurtful things someone did to you or said to you. An unforgiving person is always nervous and irritated, and he goes through a slow process of suicide. A forgiving person improves his health and eliminates many problems.

Every night at the time of sleep or at sunset, take a few minutes to forgive those who hurt you. Start with your wife, husband, boyfriend, girlfriend, or associates and say to God, "Please let my love embrace all of them."

In the Bible it says, "Revenge is Mine." The Law of Karma will take care of things, so do not look for revenge. When you try to take revenge, you create more karma, and you are entangled. Let things go, and you will feel happier.

3. Certain glands do not function properly when you have non-forgiving thoughtforms in your mind. Whatever part of your body is related to a particular thoughtform, that part of your body suffers. For example, when a person insults you or hurts you and

you watch, say, his eyes or mouth or hand movements, you create a similar tension within yourself through your hatred. This tension will later focus itself in your body in the same location which you hated most in that person's expressions.

Suppose you hated his eyes most. You will identify with the expressions of his eyes and impose on your own eyes the image of the expression of his eyes. This will cause disturbances in the aura of your eyes by imposing a new and violent image on them. The tension you create between this new image and the natural aura of your eyes will cause temporary or even permanent damage to your eyes.

A gland and an etheric center are related to every part of your body. The disturbed point in your body will affect the center, the center will affect the gland, and the gland will affect the organ.

Those who try to hurt you will have no effect upon you if you respond to them with love, forgiveness, and understanding. It is your irritation, hatred, and unforgiveness that make them effective and harmful to you.

4. Because of non-forgiveness, your mental concentration suffers terribly and you make many mistakes. You forget even simple things, such as where you placed your pencil or a piece of paper. What is happening? That thoughtform is hurting your brain and preventing you from concentrating on important things. If you have an unforgiving, revengeful, or hateful thoughtform, watch your mental behavior and see how it suffers.

5. The attitude of a person is affected by a painful event, and that event controls most of his judgments and relationships. For example, if a man gets angry at his boss and there is hatred between them, he goes home to his wife and children and shows irritation or indifference to them, poisoning all his relations with them as well.

6. Non-forgiveness gives you a false idea of perfection. When you hate someone else, it gives you a false idea that you are perfect. For example, if someone hurts you, you hate him and criticize him because you think that he is doing wrong and you are doing right. When you have such an attitude established in your mind, you think that you are the best one ever created. Because of your attitude, life will react and beat you until you learn to be forgiving, to practice right human relations, and to see exactly what you are.

In the booklet, *Light on the Path*, a great Teacher says that if you think that the sins of another person are not yours, you are still not ready for the path of initiation. Imagine if you considered the shortcomings and mistakes of others as your own, how great a feeling of forgiveness would start in your heart. You would think, "That man who lied to me *is* me, so I am the one who is lying." With such an attitude you do not condemn, criticize, reject, or hate others, but you think scientifically and try to find the real solutions to these problems.

7. On the path of evolution, non-forgiveness ties you to the events that upset you, and you cannot proceed to higher planes. In esoteric literature there are records of those people who could not progress from the astral plane to the mental plane because of their hatred. They had to wait for many thousands of years on the astral plane until they could forgive.

If you enter the lower levels of the astral plane with your revengeful, hateful thoughtforms, you have every kind of possibility there of taking revenge on people you hate, but you are creating an illusionary world for yourself. Anything you think on the astral plane turns into fact. You can take a cannon, shoot it at someone, and destroy him. Then the next day you see that he is alive. Then you take a knife and stab him, but the next day he is there again. You are in a nightmare.

One must be careful not to be caught in self-destructive thoughtforms.

Revenge is the result of intoxication in your aura. When your aura starts to be intoxicated with your hatred and non-forgiving thoughtforms, your aura is poisoned. When it is poisoned, you develop the urge for revenge.

8. Non-forgiveness prevents you from seeing issues as they are, and you fabricate every kind of thoughtform for your own advantage. When you are non-forgiving, you think, "I don't want to understand you. Whether you are right or wrong, I hate you." Maybe that other person is saying something useful, but you are preventing yourself from seeing something there. In this way, you cut yourself off from a source of wisdom, knowledge, and experience that you could gather if you were a forgiving person.

9. Non-forgiveness creates karma which then multiplies and becomes as complicated as a huge, tangled ball of threads. Because of your hatred and non-forgiveness, you speak, think, and feel in wrong ways, in disturbed ways, or in unjust ways.

For many, it is easy to forgive in their thinking, but it is not always so easy to forgive emotionally. How can we learn forgiveness on the emotional level?

Emotional forgiveness is very easy when you start working with the imagination. Imagination works on the astral body and clears it. You may see mentally that something happened that needs to be forgiven, but the emotional body is still impressed with the picture of the event. How to erase that picture?

I used to dislike a certain man, and I could not find the reason why. So I used my imagination to imagine dramatically that he was bringing a big gift to me or saving me from a great danger. When my imagination became very vivid and emotional, the previous picture of dislike suddenly melted away.

Sometimes your logic tells you it is right to do something or not to do something, but whatever you decide, your imagination is still the winner. You are either the victim of your imagination, or you are saved by your imagination. Be careful of your imagination! Imagination is a very important tool that can heal lots of wounds in the emotional body or complicate them further if it is used negatively.

One may ask whether justice contradicts forgiveness. Unfortunately, justice is often translated as punishment, but the true meaning of justice is to cause correction, to bring equilibrium, to educate, and to transform. Justice is not punishment. Justice is a way to educate you and let you know when you are out of line. Justice teaches you how you can correct conditions so as not to create serious karma for yourself.

Forgiveness never contradicts justice. In essence, real forgiveness is not an emotional attitude. It is the understanding of the causes of behavior which bring pain and suffering and an effort to liberate the person from his own wrongdoing. Justice is the ability to see the exact causes of problems and to find the most efficient ways to annihilate causes in order to restore balance, sanity, and the spiritual morality in man.

Forgiveness does not encourage injustice. Forgiveness sees things as they are. It does not take punitive actions, but it tries to evoke the hidden factor in man to correct the situation. If justice and forgiveness cannot change a situation, Cosmic Law takes action and leads the person into those situations where he eventually learns not to misuse his mind and his body in hurting others and himself.

If forgiveness is done in the right spirit, it makes a person strengthen his life and be a useful member of society. Punishment may prevent a person from continuing his crimes, but it never teaches him how to stop his crimes. It never brings a transformation in him but only feelings of rejection and revenge, as well as various poisonous emotions. Thus the victim cannot find a way out of his crimes through punishment, but he sticks to them because of the punishment. If justice is administered in the right way, it educates him, transforms him, and makes him a useful member of society.

The tragedy is that people think that when a criminal is executed, we are through with him. This is not true. He will continue to commit crimes in his subtle bodies, and he will eventually reincarnate with the same tendencies toward crime. Unless he is reeducated and transformed in justice, the problem will remain forever.

When Christ was talking about turning the left cheek to one who smites you on the right, He was esoterically referring to the Law of Karma and suggesting to his disciples to stop the interplay of action and reaction. But Christians did not understand this; they thought He was giving advice for submission and self-denial.

The proof that some people did not even understand what they thought He said is that throughout centuries they fought real and assumed enemies in the Church or outside the Church. After reading such an explanation, a person may ask, "Then what to do? Surrender?"

My intention is not to argue with them because they are very clever in defeating you by their logic. But a few suggestions can be given to answer their question:

Did Christ say, "Love your enemies"?

Did Christ say, "Forgive"?

Did Christ say, "If they ask for your shirt, give them your jacket, too"?

If He said these words and people are His faithful followers, what would be their attitude? Either Christ was teaching defeatism, or He was talking about a Cosmic Law through which final victory is only possible. But the Law of Karma wiped out hundreds of nations who were boasting of their superiority.

A spiritual person is not living to possess the earth but to renounce it. It is easy to have billions of dollars in your pocket and live in mansions and speak about the nature of Christ without touching those points which will upset the way you live.

The great message of Christ can be summarized in three lines:

    1. Spread light and educate.

2. Love until death.

3. Learn the Will of God and obey it.

If a person is not doing these three things, he will create many reasons to attack people, to violate their freedom and try to make them forget the three principle duties of the followers of Christ. There is an immense difference between Judas and Christ. A similar difference exists between the one who is Christian and the one who follows the steps of Christ.

26

Losing Faith

One of the hindrances on the path of leadership is to lose faith in co-workers. This is a very subtle factor which needs clear consideration and observation along the following lines:

a. The advancement of the leader can be so fast that he thinks his co-workers not only are not progressing, but are even going backward, and so he loses faith in them.

b. The co-workers are really doing the best they can under the pressure of their karma, their environment, and their physical, emotional, and mental limitations. The workers are sincere and striving, and the results are accumulating in the deeper layers of their souls, but the leader is failing to see this because he is expecting outer proofs.

c. The group of co-workers is not doing well because of the pressure of the outer world; because of their physical body conditions created by the misuse of the body; because of their emotional ties; and because of a lack of mental concentration, due to the traps of false teachers and teachings.

The leader must really know about the real facts and the real condition of the group. If he miscalculates the situation, he loses his faith in the co-workers; and when he loses his faith, he naturally withdraws his magnetic energy from the group. This causes a very sad condition in the group.

For example, those who are really striving feel that the unifying, attracting energy is lacking. If this continues, they slowly give up unless they themselves have large resources of that energy. Or certain members of the group begin to force others to speed their progress and thus create reaction or panic or confusion. Or the group as a whole begins to disintegrate, in spite of the efforts of the leader to keep them together.

To keep a group together, a leader must have

1. The ability to impart to them the Teaching

2. Enthusiasm

3. Faith in the members

Very often it is easier to have the ability to teach and have enthusiasm than it is to have faith in the members. When the faith is lost, the cementing, integrating energy is lost, and the group slowly disintegrates.

The leader's faith is the nucleus that keeps the system together. It acts subjectively. If his faith is withdrawn, the leader no longer feeds the souls of people, and the personalities of the co-workers begin to develop a negative polarity.

The loss of faith may be caused by several reasons:

1. It may be caused by certain members who are involved in their personality pleasures or worldly interests to such a degree that they forget their responsibilities. The leader may generalize this condition and look at the whole group as if the group were failing.

2. The leader loses faith in himself as he faces the increasing problems of a growing group. This may happen because every growth and unfoldment exposes many hidden factors which appear as hindrances on the path, but in reality they are a part of the natural process of purification of the psyche. The leader must be able to see this and not be discouraged by temporary setbacks or problems with the co-workers.

3. The leader can be discouraged and lose his faith in the group if he really sees that pollution has penetrated into it but the members are still floating on the surface and pretending they are alive and striving disciples. This is a very sad condition. If it is true, it breaks the current of energy coming from the leader and causes disintegration in the group.

However, the leader must also have a great resource of faith in human nature, and he must put that faith into action in different forms, in different places, and with people who are more eager to follow the path.

The leader must be very careful not to walk a path of contradiction. His *no* will be *no,* and his *yes* will be *yes*. This means many things. He must have a clear view of things that are happening so as not to contradict himself in his opinions, judgments, words, and actions and also not to create contradictions in the psyche of the group. It also means that he must not live a life of double standards. Such factors can have a disintegrative effect on the group.

The leader must examine himself clearly before he condemns the group and loses his faith in the group members. Many conditions in the group come into being because of the double standards of the leader or because of his psychic disturbances and the disintegration of his focus. Remember that the leader is like the etheric body of the group, and he affects the body with the changes occurring in him.

Thus before he passes judgment, he must thoroughly examine his physical, emotional, mental, and spiritual condition. After such an examination, he can clearly see the situation of each member of the group. The Teaching puts forth a principal rule that says: Never lose faith; never give up your labor for light; have the "single eye." If this rule is followed, many difficulties on the path will be eliminated.

Those who are serving the Lord must develop *divine carelessness* against all actions and plans of darkness. The protecting Hand will be there, and karma will watch very closely. The worker knows these two inevitable forces are working together for the success of the leader on the eternal path.

Divine carelessness is an unexplainable feeling. It has joy, peace, confidence, and laughter.

Every leader has primarily three worlds to deal with. The first world is the level of his consciousness and attainments. The next world is the world of people whom he tries to lead. The world of people has its own level, its own consciousness, and its own achievements. The third world is the world of higher spheres, in whose presence he stands as an officer on duty, an officer with heavy responsibilities.

The most frustrating moments of the leader are the moments in which he cannot carry out in full capacity the plans, instructions, disciplines, and messages he wants to carry out into the field because of the limitations of people, groups, or students. Here the leader may follow one of two paths:

a. He compromises with people and gives that which they want or expect in order not to disturb them or evoke negative attitudes from them.

b. He does not compromise and does not try to please them, but he urges them into a life of discipline which seems a little harder to them. In other words, he uses his leadership in proper dosage.

When a leader is trapped by the limitations of people, he cannot continue to be a leader because he tries to please them — materially, emotionally, and mentally. A trapped leader cannot give them opportunities for new breakthroughs.

For example, a leader approaches a lady who lost her husband in a military accident and tries to mourn with her, say sweet words to her, and even give some shallow advice that she can find a new husband in the future, etc. Instead, he should talk to her about karma, the Law of Reincarnation, and discipline. Often the leader cannot do such things because he is limited by the consciousness of his people. Here he steps down from his leadership and turns into a common person.

Leadership takes place the moment you can present a new path, a new vision, a new discipline, instead of compromising with the level of the people.

It is true that when the leader does not follow the path of the level of his people, they may hate him, but this is his test. He should have the wisdom to use his leadership in such a way that he creates enough tension in his people to make them move forward, without endangering their own safety.

The leader is responsible to the Higher Worlds, under whose command he works. The president of a nation can be the president only because of his glamors or he can be there to make people have whatever they desire, or he can be there to lead people to a higher state of beingness. The leader is a link between the people and the Higher Worlds. He must lead people in such a way that the Plan of the Higher Worlds is fulfilled in them.

One of the duties of the leader is to inform his people and make them understand that he will work against the tendency of involution of their three bodies. Naturally, such a procedure will create reactions and oppositions, which can accumulate and turn into an organized treason against the leader.

The leader must teach his people to swim against the current of involutionary forces which act through their threefold lower nature and through the nature of others around them.

The leader not only evokes negative actions, feelings, and thoughts from his people but also from people who are related with them. He also evokes reactions from dark forces who then try to slow or stop evolution. But if he develops deeper wisdom and learns the subtle art of leadership, he can create an intense love in his people and make them discipline themselves under the pressure of their love for him. Love facilitates the powerful discipline offered by the will of the leader.

27
How to Work

A leader must develop an ability which is called the power of insulation. No leader can do a good job if he is bothered by his family problems, health problems, worries, anxieties, negative feelings, various concerns about financial conditions, etc. He must learn to insulate himself, at least when he is on active duty.

Emotional and mental agitations and tensions must be put aside for a while when the leader is occupied with his creative work and with his immediate tasks. Many leaders lose a great deal of time and energy because of their preoccupied mind and agitated emotions, and they produce mediocre or valueless work and create confusion in their surroundings.

It is very important that they learn the science of meditation, to be able to insulate their mind and concentrate on the job in front of them. One cannot be a leader unless he achieves a certain degree of control over his mind and insulates himself from the attacks of his personality problems.

We must remember that one cannot be a true leader until he learns to control and lead his threefold personality.

The relation of the leader to the Inner Watch is imperative. The more deeply he relates to the Inner Watch, the greater becomes his power of insulation. If this power is not attained, the leader-to-be must stay away from his position and strive for a long time through concentration, meditation, and hard labor to develop the power of insulation.

Without the power of insulation, he not only damages the work for which he is dedicated, but he also becomes a dangerous person in his environment by staying in his position out of vanity and ego.

Some leaders are affected by the opinions of antagonistic persons, and they show signs of compromise with lower values because of fear or reputation. A true leader is not affected by the opinions of others if he knows what he is doing and why he is doing it.

This does not mean that a true leader is deaf and blind toward the reactions and responses of others. First of all, he feels grateful for the positive responses, but he never feels vain. Second, he sees why some people are negative or have certain reactions.

A true leader knows that reactions are of two kinds:

1. They are based upon slander, malice, treason, jealousy, and self-interest.

2. They are based upon habits of thinking, tradition, education, and limited consciousness.

Toward the first kind of reaction, he develops extreme watchfulness. He tries to educate the people with the second kind of reaction. He does not feel hurt because of their attitude, and he fully understands them. He tries to use their reaction as an opportunity to reach them and expand their consciousness. But once he engages himself in his tasks and creative work, he insulates himself and reaches a state of divine indifference.

In the first kind of reaction, the leader knows that the enemies of the Teaching can control the Teacher only if he acknowledges their malice and slander with his own reaction. Thus, the next lesson that the leader is going to learn is divine indifference toward disturbing noise and personality reactions.

Indifference is different from insulation. Insulation is protection for your labor. Indifference is rejection of the power of reaction. Insulation is related to your personal life and family in general. Indifference is related to negative forces and their reactions.

28
Laws of Life

A law is the way things naturally go or should go, or the way people want them to go. If the life people create is not in harmony with the laws of Nature, sooner or later they will see the laws of Nature creating painful ways to make them turn to natural laws.

It is also possible that man-made laws assist Nature to carry on its evolution in a better way. This is possible because man, being a part of Nature, can create laws that are in harmony with the natural laws or are auxiliary to them.

Some of our discoveries are the result of the utilization of natural laws but are used against natural laws. Human intelligence is capable of using the natural laws against the natural laws, evoking a heavy reaction from Nature.

The speediest way to progress is to use natural laws for the purpose for which they exist.

The laws of Nature work in many dimensions — in rocks, minerals, plants, oceans, and winds; in the emotional world; in the mental world; in the moral and spiritual worlds. The laws controlling your social relationships, feelings, thinking, and aspirations are as real as the laws of science, physics, chemistry, biology, etc.

The following points are given here as seed thoughts for reflection or contemplation. Thinking on one of them and doing a reflective meditation upon it will bring many blessings to your life:

1. You eventually become like those whom you hate, and you start to act as they act.//
2. You hate someone because you hate things in him that are the process of developing within you.
3. Those who have so as to give to others, they will have more. Those who have so as to have more, they will lose what they have. One must periodically empty himself to be able to be filled afresh.
4. When one is empty of himself, the Universe will dwell in him.
5. When one is filled by his self, Satan will use him for his own enjoyment.
6. If you ask, the answer will be given. If you knock, people will respond. If you search, things will come your way.
7. Those who spread dirt eventually find it as their nourishment.
8. Those who waste your offerings will also make you indebted to the Creator.
9. Your body is the result of your actions or labor.
10. Your emotional body is the result of your words, imagination, and emotional reactions.
11. Your mental body is the result of your thoughts, visualizations, or vanity and ego.
12. Your body of glory is the result of your service to

Light, Beauty, Goodness, Righteousness, Joy, and Freedom.

13. Beauty evokes seeds of beauty latent in you.

14. Nothing is lost in the Universe.

15. No one can change things for the better or cause transformation unless *he exists* or obeys *one who exists*.

16. There is the law of opposites. Light evokes darkness; darkness evokes light.

17. Each person accumulates a savings by his good deeds. When the time for payment of his own past bad deeds arrives, his savings intervenes.

18. In linking yourself with higher powers, you enter into the sphere of their protection.

19. There is the law of substitution by which you are allowed to pay the debts of others.

20. Your payment for others becomes your savings.

21. Those whose debt is paid help you in your future achievements.

22. Only after you empty yourself can you be filled.

23. Success is the result of the exhaustion of karma.

24. Suffering removes a great amount of karma.

25. Accumulated unconscious impressions create pressure within us. One of Nature's ways to make us conscious of them is to see them in others.

26. We are afraid of people whom we hate.

27. We hate because we feel insecure.

28. Racism and nationalism are the result of fear and insecurity.

29. Bigots and fanatics are those who had extreme fear in the past because of their faith.

30. Harmlessness leads to freedom from any limitations.

31. No value can exist unless it is realized and actualized.

32. No value can be realized unless vehicles to realize that value are built or created.

33. The transmitting agent conditions the nature of the transmission.

34. One reaches the ocean of values not by imitating or living in the values of others, but by creating his own values on progressively higher levels and in a more inclusive nature.

35. Expansion of consciousness occurs after crises and high-level tensions if one is in the light.

36. The things that we possess by force are the things that we will lose in pain and suffering.

37. Knowledge is like acid. It burns its surroundings unless it is in the cup of love.

38. The power to possess and dominate is a sign of bankruptcy of essence and a preparation for karmic retribution.

39. Enemies conquered by force are those who in the future will incarnate in the conquering nation and lead it toward destruction.

40. There is only one Nature. Ignorance creates the supernatural.

41. The Law of Life demands that you do your best in whatever you are doing. The "will-to-do-your-best" must be ever-progressive.

42. The ultimate goal of thinking is to understand the Law behind the Universe.

43. Love and respect are the best ways to cultivate the things within you that you love and respect in others.

44. A good relation with God cannot be achieved without having a good relation with His children.

LAWS

1. All units, formed or in formation, on any level or in any form, evoke hostile attacks from their environment which try to disintegrate them.

2. Every form built for the service of humanity has its invisible protector, if the form continues to live for the Purpose.

3. If you put a burden on a consciousness which is not ready to be burdened, the consciousness rejects it or distorts it.

4. Those who do not share, lose what they have.

5. Those who hide themselves from their own light will never be able to find their True Self.

6. Those who allow themselves to be eaten by elementals will soon disappear in them.

7. There are two poles which control a person's action — vision and self-interest. If vision controls the person, he advances. If self-interest controls, he degenerates.

8. People leak energy when they react to the personality attitudes of others.

9. Selflessness is a way to prevent reaction.

10. Perseverance is a chain of continuous effort which takes you from the limitation of time to the freedom of timelessness.

11. Successful families, groups, and nations are built only on the foundation of trust.

12. If you want to grow, make your horizon wider and do not try to narrow the horizons of others.

13. We build abscesses in our mental body by not feeling sorry for the deeds that we did to hurt others.

14. Creativity is an effort to contact the hearts of others.

15. Once a person actualizes a virtue, that virtue does not exist any more for him; it becomes a part of his nature, not something outside him.

16. When there is tension between two members in a group, it is better not to give any position or labor to either of them.

For example, if two people hate each other and if one of them sings, the other person will project negative emotions and thoughts within the group and contaminate the group. If one gives a lecture, the other party will misinterpret his words and send out disturbing thoughts.

Experience shows that both must be sacrificed until harmony is achieved between them.

17. Many great labors are destroyed when co-workers begin to make personality demands on each other. Real workers are those who can sacrifice their personality demands for the sake of the spiritual labor.

18. Fanaticism is a proof that a person is caught in his own trap.

There are laws that have two sides, without which the law will not exist. For example, two important laws are

1. Do not discriminate against those of different races or national origins, nor emphasize your own nation or your own race.

Racial discrimination is forbidden. This is one side. But what about those who strongly emphasize their nationalism? Isn't that an imposition of their nationalism on others and a way to tell others they are different? The law will be complete if we add to it: Nationalistic activities and propaganda when done to hurt or exclude others, are a direct violation of the law of "non-racial discrimination."

2. Leave others free to worship God according to their beliefs and faith, and do not push your own religion as the only way or the best way.

Under the law of freedom of religion, everyone is free to worship God according to his own beliefs and faith. This is one side of the law. The other side is that no one must profess that his religion is the "only way to fly." This will be a direct violation of the above law and an act of discrimination.

29

The Three Enemies of the Leader-to-Be

Vanity, showing off, and ego are three serious enemies of the leader-to-be.

Vanity must be uprooted from our nature because it creates negativity and eliminates the magnetism of the leader. One should continuously watch his thoughts, emotions, words, and actions to see if they carry a certain dosage of vanity. Such an observation will pave the way for future success. Vanity puts your building on false foundations.

Showing off is a manipulative technique, and it creates rejection from those who are ready to enter the path. Showing off must be eliminated by all means because it uses the energy of the Self and creates a false "I." The person emphasizes his false "I."

"I did it.... I am doing it.... I have it.... I have done it," etc. All activities of such a person turn around his false self.

Showing off is mostly manifested through our words when we subtly want to manipulate a person and use him for our advantage. This is so subtle that one must develop eagle eyes to observe it.

Showing off does not let higher energies flow in.

Showing off also manifests in trying to draw the attention of people to what you are doing or what you are. It is not easy to make people appreciate others when you have a craving to take the credit. We must try to enjoy the appreciation given to others and even sometimes be indifferent toward any praise given to us.

Once, before I was going to take a very serious responsibility in the temple, my Teacher told me to bring to his office the book I had written about the soul. When I went there, I found many Teachers sitting around a table. When I entered, one of the Teachers said, "Oh, that is the book you wrote."

I felt very embarrassed and became red.

"Well," said another Teacher, "tell us how you wrote it."

I looked at my Teacher and said, "It is his ideas and visions and thoughts that I tried to collect. But no matter what I did, I don't feel that I did justice to my Teacher."

"But that is your book, isn't it so?" asked another Teacher.

"The book would be mine if I had conceived the ideas found in the book. But all the ideas were given to me by my Teacher — although who knows how much distortion can be found in it. I can sincerely say that only the distortions belong to me."

"Can you burn it if your Teacher wants you to burn it?"

"Yes, of course."

I looked at my Teacher, ready for his command.

"Here is the stove," he said. "Throw it in." And I threw in my manuscript which I had worked on for three years, day and night. After I saw it burning, I went and hugged my Teacher.

"Do you feel sorry?"

"No," I said, "as long as you are my Teacher."

They let me go to my room. I felt so released and happy. For twenty-one days they waited to see if I spoke about the event to anyone, but I did not. On the twenty-second day, they invited me again to an Ashram. The rest is personal.

Try to develop extreme humility; avoid showing off.

Vanity, showing off, and ego are a trinity. They work together but have different offices. Ego manifests in hurt feelings and in imposition of one's own desires upon others. Ego is separative, aloof, and self-contained. Ego works, talks, and thinks only if his self-interest is met or guaranteed. He is satisfied only if he is fed.

Ego has a tendency to occupy greater and greater territories at the expense of others. Ego has an intellectual dishonesty. He tries to shine dressed in the colorful feathers of the values of others and thus always keeps himself on the surface.

The leader-to-be must cultivate selflessness. This has very deep layers of meaning, but let us take one of them.

Selflessness is the ability to remove your ego, with all its wealth, from the path so that the higher energies flow through you. How to remove the ego? Thinking and feeling that all Beauty, Goodness, Righteousness, Joy, Freedom, and creativity are the gifts of the Higher Powers and you are only a witness of the works done through you will remove the ego and lead you to selflessness.

Once you understand this, you will discover by yourself the other layers of selflessness.

For all successes, feel grateful to the Higher Powers. For all failures, see the interferences of your personality and personality concerns.

When one begins to boast and feel hilarious for a success or victory, he repulses the presence of higher forces and replaces himself on the throne. One must develop the awareness that all higher gifts are manifested through him from the One Self.

Fear of failure is a sign of identification with ego. There will be no failure if you let the higher energies work through you, without any friction from your personality.

The ego thinks in terms of success and failure. The Self thinks only to do his task. The greatest success is the performance of tasks — not the results.

30

Leadership and Warnings

The leadership must always be in a position to see dangers and warn the co-workers.

This is sometimes a hard and unpleasant work, but it is one of the labors which makes the individual and group advance.

People are surrounded with dangers, but they are unaware of them. And because they are not conscious of them, they are in grave danger, which means

— they may lose their health

— they may lose their sanity

— they may lose their happiness and joy

— they may lose their social position

— they may lose their moral and spiritual standards

— they may lose all that they have

There are even dangers which will destroy their happiness in the subtle worlds and paralyze them in their future incarnations. But most of the contemporary leaders are blind to these dangers.

Contemporary leaders fall into the following categories:

1. They are blind to dangers.

2. They are in darkness.

3. They know about the dangers but they underestimate them.

4. They are afraid to talk about dangers so as not to upset their income.

5. They have an attitude of bribery and flattery, showing only what is rosy to their followers.

6. They are like the one who every minute shouts, "Wolves are coming. Prophesies of destruction are upon us," thus using fear techniques to make people hide their head in the leader's pocket.

7. Then there are those leaders who are clearly aware of danger and warn their co-workers. They know how and when and in what dosage to talk about danger to arouse courage, daring, striving, and discipline. They let their co-workers see the danger that is confronting them without paralyzing their actions and without creating fear and panic. These leaders help their followers take courageous actions to avoid the danger and use it as an opportunity to raise their consciousness and increase the productivity of their labor.

The Great Sage says, "In the face of danger, human forces are multiplied in tension; likewise, the state of ecstasy produces an influx of super earthly forces. If such a tension is established, it is then possible to prolong this moment — in other words, man may receive a continuous increase of forces."

What are the dangers about which the leader will make his co-workers aware? Let us mention a few of them:

— Physical dangers coming from polluted water, radiated food, preservatives, polluted air.

- Dangers from prostitution, drugs, alcohol, wrong relationships, sexually transmissible diseases, earthquakes.
- Emotional dangers of hate, fear, anger, jealousy, revenge, irritation.
- Mental dangers of separatism which lead to wars, murders, crimes, destruction.
- Dangers from earthquakes, fires, and other catastrophes.
- Dangers of ego which lead to exploitation in any form.
- Dangers of vanity which prevent expansion of consciousness.
- Dangers of false teachings and teachers which cause mental insanity, emotional disturbance, and physical illness. The condition of the mind reflects on the condition of the body.
- Dangers coming from mediums, channels, lower psychics, because they are contact lines between lower astral and etheric planes and humanity. They are often channels of dark forces. They are those who bring massive obsession and possession.
- Dangers from immorality which opens the door to obsession and possession.
- Dangers from overstimulation.
- Dangers from hypnotism.
- Dangers from dark forces which are like "lions waiting to devour us."
- Dangers from manipulators who manipulate not only average citizens but also big companies, big groups of

people, churches, and various departments of the government to exploit people for their unending greed.

— Dangers from hypocrites, gossipers, slanderers, traitors, from those who approach you as wolves in sheep's skin.

If the leader opens his eyes he will see all these, and hundreds of other dangers, and realize that his co-workers are walking on barrels full of explosives.

The leader's duty is first to be fearless, in the faith that he will be protected from all these dangers as long as he puts his heart in the flame of the Hierarchy.

His next duty is to watch and observe each of his co-workers and friends and make them aware of the danger as much as they can handle it. And when they are aware, he must teach them how to handle the dangers, how to fight against them, what devices or weapons to use against them, how to mobilize forces against them, and how to fight them without fear, without vanity, and how not to overdo or go beyond what he can do.

Fighting against dangers is a supreme art, and only a true leader knows how to do it and how to teach it.

If a leader cannot see dangers waiting on the way of his co-workers, he is a traitor to his sacred duty of leadership.

One must know that on every step people are in danger — physical danger, moral danger, spiritual danger — and only a leader can warn about a danger and show the way to conquer or to avoid it.

The leader's intention in pointing out the dangers is not to create cowards, invalids, nor to create dependency on others, nor to create people who are obsessed by the idea of danger every moment of their life. The leader's intention is to create

1. Warriors, fighters

2. Those who can surf on dangers

3. Those who can eliminate the "snakes" that poison people

4. Those who can use their intelligence or heart qualities to stop the epidemics of insanity

5. Those who can stand against armies and defend the interests of one humanity

6. Those who are ready to sacrifice their lives for the principles on which are built great cultures and the future humanity

The leader wants his followers to be healthy, balanced, serene, intelligent, in control, spiritual, heroic, highly educated, creative, fearless, daring, and striving.

He wants them crowned by the diamond of all virtues — but having a head of humility and simplicity.

Once the dangers are known and intelligently confronted, the new warrior will feel the ecstasy which comes to him as a current of gratitude from those Invisible Ones who see "things as they are" in the world and who rejoice upon seeing the emergence of new warriors.

The security of an individual, the security of a nation, the security of humanity depend on knowing the dangers and being prepared to handle the dangers in such a way that the world security is not undermined. Then even the agents of dangers and darkness are transformed and become helpful elements in the society of the world.

The warriors of the Future are not fanatics of religious or political doctrines and dogmas.

The warriors of the Future are not embodiments of greed, racism, and nationalism.

The warriors of the Future are not experts of the killing arts or of the sciences of destruction.

The warriors of the Future are not liars, imitators, exploiters, manipulators. The warriors of the Future are

— Illuminators

— Healers

— Transformers

— Way openers

They are those who expand our consciousness, who put our heart in contact with the Cosmic Heart to create harmony, cooperation, unity, and synthesis.

The warriors of the Future are pioneers of the Higher Worlds, the spiritual realms. They fight against darkness, death, disease, ignorance, separatism, and greed.

It is a great honor to be a warrior of the Future because each true warrior will be a transmitter of the light, love, beauty, and bliss which will flow in from higher realms of the Universe and regenerate the life of this suffering planet.

People think that a leader must lead people the way the people want to be led. The Teaching says that the leader must not follow the lead of the people but, instead, lead them. How will he lead them? Not by the force of his military power and authority, but by the power of his vision, intelligence, and intuition!

The leader stands between two worlds. One world is beauty, vision, and the Higher Worlds. The other world is the world of people's desires, inclinations, habits, and ignorance. The leader's duty is to make people sensitive to beauty, to higher values and higher visions, and to the Higher Worlds. He will do this by using three techniques:

1. Education

2. Wisdom

3. Power

The more the public is educated, the closer it will be to harmony and right relations. Wisdom means to be educated about cause and effect in the individual and collective life and on the three levels of the human personality. Power is to be used to protect the public against itself. The first expression of power is law.

Leadership is like a mother taking care of a child so that the child

1. Grows in a healthy way

2. Is protected from serious dangers

3. Does not think in ways that are against his future development and responsibilities

4. Is led to the path of harmonious development

5. Finds the state in which he can stand on his own feet and contribute to the welfare of the nation and of humanity

If we choose a leader and want him to act exactly under our will and desire, then there is no need for a leader. Such a leader will be forced to organize the members of the nation collectively to live the way they want in license. Such a leadership ends in chaos.

We must choose a leader who is qualified for leadership. Leadership is the midwife of the visions of your Soul, the midwife of the inner spiritual drives, dreams, and urges to achieve spiritual perfection. A true leader is sensitive to the visions of your Soul. He works with them and even sometimes against your personality inclinations, glamors, and illusions.

Democracy in its true sense is the ability to create a close, cooperative relationship between the leadership and the highest visions of your Soul. When this cooperation is factualized, democracy recognizes your individual freedom in the sense that it hurts neither your efforts to achieve the vision of your Soul nor the efforts of humanity to achieve the vision of its Soul.

A democratic leader knows about the vision. He knows about the degree of ability you have at the present to achieve that vision. He knows how to regulate the speed by which you run toward that goal. He knows how to expose the enemies of your progress. He knows how to help you to recover from your failures on the path. He knows how to stop you at the edge of a precipice.

He knows how to encourage certain groups to act as forerunners and examples for your future achievements. He knows how to evoke in you a desire to progress forward on the path of perfection by demonstrating in his own life the life of a hero who achieved and left behind the harvest as nourishment for multitudes.

One of the most important qualities of leadership is *integrity*. Integrity means that the leaders of an organization, government, or any group must work as if they were one man. Any separative or separate plan, expression, or action works against this integrity and the leadership disintegrates.

The whole strength and power of any organization rests in this integrity.

The leaders can think differently; they can have different ways to achieve a goal and different speeds and times, but such differences must not make them take separate actions. Behind any action of the group there must exist a unanimous decision. Until such a decision is reached, action must not be taken.

There can be opposing viewpoints and alternate viewpoints. These are all natural and beneficial, but they must not be motive powers to an action without a unanimous decision to act.

All differences must be *digested* by the leadership. They must be harmonized and correlated, and a synthesis must be achieved. Only then must action be carried out. Anything that hurts the integrity of the leadership must be carefully avoided. Those groups, organizations, and governments that last longer are those that function under the law of integrity. Whenever integrity suffers, the danger of disintegration sets in.

The health of human beings, as well as the health of groups, organizations, and governments is measured through the degree of their integrity. Integrity does not mean totalitarianism and power politics in the leadership itself. Integrity is the result of intuitive understanding of the need and problem and an ability to synthesize various viewpoints until they present an integrated approach or action which both meets the need and uses the various ideas in harmony.

Leaders are very attractive to dark forces. Dark forces are always after a leader who spreads good. They have many tools to catch a leader. They have the net, the hook, and explosives. The net symbolizes the reputation and the honors in which some leaders are caught. The hook symbolizes the glamors in their many forms which create attachments in them. The explosives symbolize the illusions whose bases are all kinds of ideas related to separatism. With these three tools, the dark forces make the leaders involved, attached, separative, and make them fail.

The consciousness of a leader-to-be must be disciplined so that he does not run after reputation, fame, praise, or flattery. The consciousness of the leader must be trained in order not to be stuck in glamors. Glamors are desires which are blown up or dramatized through imagination. Illusions are truths and facts prostituted by selfishness and enslaved by personal interests.

Every great spiritual leader is indifferent toward building his reputation. He does his job and does not expect people to praise him. He even feels very uncomfortable when people start praising him.

He also tries not to create attachments because he knows that attachments will sap his energy which he needs for his job.

He also tries not to fall into illusions because he knows that illusions will distract him, mislead him, and eventually make his labor useless.

Traps may be laid on the path of a leader. He can pass over these traps by always thinking that he is a servant doing his job for the Lord and that the Lord, Himself, is working through him.

31

Writing Letters

It is an art to write letters. Of course, there are many kinds of letters, written for many different purposes, but all of them must have two fundamental characteristics: simplicity and clarity.

My mother used to say, "Remember, you are not there with your reader to help him understand your letter." Those who read your letters are affected by your psychic energy, by your logic and thoughts, and by your words and message. This means that at the time you write the letter, you must be charged with psychic energy. If you are not in a charged state, before you write the letter you must charge yourself through prayer, meditation, and silence.

Your thoughts must be clear and to the point. It is very important to formulate your thoughts in those words and expressions that clearly reflect the depth of your thoughts. Clear statements of your thoughts carry the charge of your mental energy. Also, you must not be carried away by your own knowledge and level but consider the knowledge and level of the one to whom you are writing.

The formations of your sentences and the words you choose make a great difference. Some people show in their letters that they know words that are not commonly used. Such letters create reactions from the reader. Unless it is imperative to use sophisticated words, use the simple ones and build clear sentences to express exactly what you want to say. Do not try to impress your reader that you know lots of words.

It is also ugly to advertise yourself in your letters and try to impress your reader. People must feel your sincerity, simplicity, and clarity in all your expressions. Do not complicate your sentences with clauses, dashes, etc.

One of the most important things to put in your letters is optimism. Optimism creates a good response.

Let us consider business letters. Suppose you are asking someone to pay a past-due bill for which you have already sent several reminders. One efficient way to write such a letter is to send a simple statement saying, "We are expecting you to pay your bill (specify). Most sincerely yours . . . ." Then you may enclose a statement listing the reminders of the bill due by their dates sent. A third page may be enclosed, giving the purpose of the mutual business:

Dear Sir,

We need your business, and we are sure you are happy with our business; but we need our customers to pay their bills so that we are able to keep our business running in the proper way. We are sure you will help us to be more efficient in our relationship.

Yours truly,

Signature

These three enclosures will give a clear picture of your attitude:

1. Payment due
2. Past history
3. Future prospects

Here are more examples that can be used in various businesses:

FIRST LETTER:

Dear Sir,

Please send us three gallons of eucalyptus oil with your bill.

Yours truly,

Signature

SECOND LETTER:

Dear Sir,

These are the dates we wrote to you and received no answers: (List dates)

No signature

THIRD LETTER:

Dear Sir,

We want very much to receive your product for the benefit of our customers and for the mutual benefit of your firm and our firm. We anticipate that you will consider our order and take immediate action to deliver it.

Yours truly,

Signature

In your letters to your friends, students, or co-workers you must show the spirit of joy and enthusiasm. People must feel that your thoughts are fresh and youthful. You must demonstrate courage and daring. Such letters carry a great charge of energy, strengthen people, and challenge them to greater service and dedication.

Joyfulness inspires people and puts their higher energies in action. It repels stagnation and brings into the group new, refreshing, regenerating energies. Joyfulness dispels negative accumulations within our aura and environment and thus prevents dark forces from taking advantage of the negative atmosphere to prepare attacks upon us. Not only in your letters but also during your conversations, try to keep your voice sonorous and joyful.

It is also very important to impart hope in your letters. Hope is a power which sees things improving in the future. Hope brings into actualization the things which are seen as improved in the future. Thus, charge your letters and talks with hope, with the spirit of positivism and enthusiasm.

Never use fanaticism in your letters. Fanaticism is a sign of deterioration. Before a fanatic starts to destroy his crystallized thoughtforms, he increases in heat. The heat rises to such a degree that eventually it destroys the formations of crystallized thoughts and he is free. But this freedom manifests in two main forms. First, the fanatic may suddenly feel like he is in a vacuum wherein he loses all his support and falls into deep layers of depression. Second, the fanatic passes through a storm of gradually increasing confusion and finally feels free and peaceful, realizing that he is out of a nightmare that now he can lead a life of freedom in the spirit of cooperation and striving.

It is a crime to lead the reader of your letter into fanaticism, just as it is a crime to imprison a bird in a cage. Always leave the doors and windows of your thoughts open so that your guests feel the freedom of Mother Nature.

Never try to confuse your readers. Never try to make them believe you or follow you. It is your sincerity, enthusiasm, hope, and youthfulness of spirit that will evoke their souls — and that is all that you need.

Another very important thing for the leader to do is to keep regular and accurate records of all his activities. These records must be kept monthly, and every year they must be filed for future reference. The records must include

- interviews
- counselling
- meetings
- seminars
- conventions
- speeches
- compositions
- rehearsals
- travel
- letters written
- ceremonies
- radio or television appearances
- publications
- buildings
- articles

This will be easier to do if the leader has a notebook in which to record his daily activities. This will be the record of his visible labor.

32

Leadership Defined

Leadership is not position or power but an influence that orients people toward the path of perfection through Beauty, Goodness, Righteousness, Joy, and Freedom. This influence is like a pouring, expanding light, which has a source and a field. This field of light can expand as the light increases and help more and more people find the path of perfection and learn how to strive on that path.

Leadership is like a link in a chain. One link is the vision, the magnet, which evokes striving and which reveals great spiritual values and principles. The other link is the field of service, the field of influence, and the field of actualization of spiritual achievements. A leader will not be effective in either one of these fields separately; he exists only in relation to these two fields. His teaching and his guidance always relate these two fields.

Being an influential soul, a leader must not serve the personality interests of people without serving, in the meantime, their spiritual progress. Only through cultivating the spiritual interests of people can one properly serve their personality needs.

Some people, after experiencing the power of spiritual principles, try to teach them to others, but only to use these principles to increase their own wealth, to gain position, to increase their ego, and to enjoy pleasures. This is called spiritual prostitution. It leads one farther and farther from the spiritual path.

A real leader emphasizes first the "Kingdom of God." It is after this realization that the true leader presents higher principles and laws.

Leadership will never serve special interests. It is possible that, because of his influence, special or separative interest groups will approach him to use his power, wisdom, talents, and influence for their own interests. If a leader is used for special interests, that ends his leadership.

The purpose of leadership is not to increase cleavages between parties or to make them individually wealthy and strong but to fuse their interests and charge people with striving toward greater spiritual values.

Once a great man came to a town and a businessman tried by all means to have his picture taken with the great man. He was refused. One day, while the great man was being led to his car, the cook came out and kissed his hand. Then the cook asked if his son could take a picture of them both. The great man, with a big smile, agreed, and the picture was taken.

For days I thought about the depth of consciousness of such a great man. Real leaders are proud enough not to allow people to use them, but also humble enough to give joy to those who have pure love and devotion.

Leadership is not only influence but also the fruit of your labor. The greater the field of your influence, the greater your service and the greater your leadership, provided that such a leadership produces the fruits of Beauty, Goodness, Righteousness, Joy, and Freedom.

You will be called a true leader not because so many people followed your steps but because so many people were led toward a higher state of consciousness and brought with them abundant fruits because of your labor.

If we had a computer that would register all the changes that you brought into the consciousness and into the life of people on the path of improvement and perfection, the sum total of them will proclaim the kind of leader you are.

By their fruits you will know them, not especially the fruits of the leader but the fruits of all the "trees" that the leader cared for.

Sometimes the influence of a leader survives beyond the length of his life, and even beyond the memory of his immediate people.

Influence, like a wave of electricity, travels not only in the physical life of many, but it goes beyond it and becomes active in subtle planes too.

33

Leadership and Ideas

In the minds of people leadership is related to multitudes and to a person who rules them, controls them, or directs them. But real leadership is not connected to multitudes or to groups of people but to ideas. People have to realize that it is the ideas that lead people and the world. The higher and more inclusive the idea, the better is the leadership.

In the future, people will realize that leaders are broadcasters, carriers, embodiments, or even symbols of ideas.

A leader is a true leader when he presents an idea which meets the needs of people in the present and in the future and leads them on a path of progressive advancement.

Real leaders in the past moved and guided multitudes, not with their might and power but by their ideas. Often, behind the kings and queens, behind any prominent leader, stood a *wise man*. It was the ideas of a wise man that ruled a nation, although presented by the apparent leader. Wise men led nations from behind a "curtain," not in front of the multitudes or by wearing a crown.

An idea provides those means and ways through which the needs of people are met, the vision of the future is presented, and issues of the present are revealed.

Leadership without living ideas is a force which is based on self-interest and vanity. This force can organize multitudes and orchestrate them into certain activities which meet the vanities, glamors, and egos of people. But it does not help people flourish or expand their consciousness, and it does not help them live in the light of the One Self.

Such organized multitudes become a curse for a nation because they present a crystallized thoughtform and not living ideas.

A leader knows that an idea is "the seed of reality." It is this seed that is planted in the hearts of people to enrich them with the abundance of reality.

People have various definitions about the word "reality." In the Teaching, *reality* is defined as the *cause* of existing forms, whether they are physical, emotional, or mental. Reality is an archetype which manifests in many layers, with varying magnitudes and shades. An idea does not present these shades and magnitudes but only the original archetype, the cause.

An idea in any field of human endeavor or human relationship is a path leading to progressive advancement toward the archetypal state. Harmony comes into being when an idea materializes in many fields and advances the fields toward the archetype.

Those who try to rule by the power of force, threat, prowess, flattery, and bribery; those who try to rule by providing all that is necessary to satisfy people's egos, glamors, and pleasures are those who plant the seeds of the future destruction of the nation.

Leadership nourishes people with life-giving ideas which lead them progressively forward toward beauty, harmony, enlightenment, and synthesis.

A true leader is a spring of new ideas. It is through ideas that he leads people. Force and might, position and power crystallize people in their lower natures and in the interests therein. Ideas speak to the human soul, once the ears of the human soul are open.

Human souls are attracted to each other only after perceiving life-giving ideas. Cooperation between human souls is only possible in the light and beauty of ideas.

People charged by living ideas march toward building a new world grounded in living ideas.

It is ideas that tune people to the source of Cosmic energies. Cosmic energies flow into the ocean of humanity through living ideas.

The bond between the Highest Source and human beings is established only through living ideas and through actualization of those ideas.

How can a man advance to his Source if there is no leader to show the path? The path is shown through the ideas which a leader offers to the multitudes.

Every true idea is a messenger of the Most High.

People look to Krishna, Buddha, and Christ as greater Leaders and powerful individuals in world history. But, in reality, They are not individuals but embodiments of Cosmic Ideas. They are words — ideas — "made flesh."

Once a Soul becomes an embodiment of a Cosmic Idea, He turns into a continuous and everlasting source of energy in the sphere of existence. He becomes a distributing and broadcasting source in Space which, like a beacon, leads nations to a safe destination.

The thoughts of every great leader are nothing else but interpretations of ideas and their *appropriation* to life's demands.

Thus the Teachings of the Great Ones are symphonies composed upon great ideas.

When a living idea is received in one's soul, it reveals the beauty of relationships existing between the idea and the fires in Space. Every true idea ignites the fires of Space and creates a network of fire, which eventually turns into a magnetic mirror attracting Cosmic Ideas.

In the future, people must not be led by might, by fear and threats, but by life-giving ideas. All the misery of crime, theft, exploitation, deception, and dishonesty are the result of false leadership, the result of leadership based on fear, threat, and might. No society will enter the path of honesty under fear, threat, and might because these elements will nourish the seeds of crime.

True leadership is leadership by ideas which present vision and future.

Ideologies, dogmas, and doctrines are the funeral ceremonies of slaughtered ideas. True living ideas do not create ideologies, theologies, dogmas, and doctrines. They continuously destroy crystallization, regimentation, concretization.

Ideas are the flowers of energies.

Any effort to imprison an idea into a theology, ideology, dogma, or doctrine makes it vanish and leave only dying forms behind.

An idea is not a form, neither is it a formulation, but a living stream of energy connecting you with the Source of an ever-flowing waterfall of energy and vision.

An idea releases the power of striving in people.

A real thought is not a thoughtform. A real thought is the factual unfoldment of an idea and the process of its adjustment to the needs of life. Thus, a real thought makes the idea effective for the problems of humanity by relating it to as many points of necessity as possible. But no thoughtform can fully embody an idea.

If an idea does not create the power of striving, it is not an idea but a thoughtform.

Thoughtforms are temporary stepping stones to help you cross the river. The power of striving is an incessant labor toward perfection. How can it be otherwise when an idea is a link between you and the Highest?

True ideas never disappear even if they are imprisoned in ideologies, theologies, dogmas, and doctrines. They leave their prisons on any plane or level and ascend to higher spheres. At the right moment, charged with higher spheres, they return again to the world of man to destroy the idols people created upon the original ideas.

Leadership in the world eventually will turn into a network of electrical wires through which the Cosmic Ideas will freely circulate, gradually pulling all kingdoms toward their divine Archetypes.

34

Leadership and Motives

One of the leaders-to-be presented a question: "Do you think a leader must ever reject a service which a person wants to render?"

I feel that you should not accept a service behind which lurks a malicious or dishonest motive. If you cannot see the motive, observe the one who is in the process of serving you and try to find it.

You can discover his motive by talking with him and finding out where he served previously, why he quit there, and what problems he encountered. If you find that his motive is grey, discontinue his service immediately and put him in the spotlight of your steady observation.

The second method used to discover motive is to show dissatisfaction in what he is doing as a service to such a degree that you create anger and upset his emotional balance. Then watch his physical, emotional, and mental reactions.

The third method is steadily to change his job and watch his different reactions and relationships.

The fourth method is to try to find his goals in life.

The questioner continued: "If you know that someone's motive is bad but you are in an emergency, do you reject his help?"

My method is to reject his help, because by rejecting his help you are honest with yourself and you do not encourage his motive by letting him take advantage of your situation. Remember that those who have evil motives will wait until you are in an emergency so that they can control you by exploiting your weakness.

"Then the questioner asked: "If we do not know the motive of a person, should we reject his help in an emergency?"

Of course not, but after he helps you, express gratitude but do not surrender to him or give him a permanent job until you know much, much more about him and about his past.

Some people have mixed motives. As a leader, you can change their motives and lead them toward the right path. Such a person can be handled in the following ways:

1. Give him basic duties and encourage him toward selfless service.

2. Keep him at the same job a long time and do not promote him. Observe his patience, his joy in work, and his willingness to cooperate.

3. If he gains your acceptance, let him teach his job to someone else or to a few people. Have close contact with those who have been taught. Then make him do something more basic.

Through watching his attitude you can see if any traces of wrong motive remain in him. Once you are convinced of the person's faithfulness or honesty, you can raise his position. Sometimes people reveal themselves in higher positions very quickly and expose their motives easily.

The underlying message in these methods is that one should not be glamored by those who offer service. Be careful, especially of those who express words like

"I am under your command."

"I can do anything you want."

"You just tell me what to do, and then leave me alone to do it."

"I can do better than X-Y-Z. You must have confidence in me."

Beyond these four statements, be careful of those who

1. Flatter you

2. Bribe you with gifts

3. Try to show off in various ways, for example, in using sophisticated stationery, dressing, or bragging about their talent

Apart from such people, there are others who very eagerly want to help but who are not ready or fit for work.

You must also be very careful of

1. Drug users

2. Psychiatric patients

3. Those with past records of crime and insanity

4. Those who fall in love with you unconditionally or without serious reason

5. Those who want to build a name or position for themselves

6. Those who use service to show off

7. Those who lack solemnity

Remember that a leader learns from his failures if he has standards or principles. Remember also that certain failures are fatal, and a leader loses so much time and energy trying to recover himself.

There are also those who like to involve themselves in your work by

1. Lending important equipment, money, or their talents.
2. Giving you things to use, stating that you can use them as long as you need them.

Such people may have wrong motives.

They may want to be a part of your work so they use their money, equipment, furniture, or credentials for admittance.

They maneuver to take higher positions or to penetrate into the secrets of your business, even eventually trying to take over.

They try to remove certain persons who are potential dangers to their future plans, or they remove such a servant to make you depend more on them.

They may associate your work with groups or organizations that have bad reputations.

Some people show cooperation in order to take many responsibilities on their shoulders. This is not with the intention of helping you but of gaining power over you and making you meet their increasing demands. They do this because they think, "The leader will collapse if I withdraw all my engagements and responsibilities." The leader must be careful not to depend on one person to do many duties but to leave several capable people so that he does not fall under anyone's control.

By lending you equipment and money, they also make you depend on them. Then at a critical time, they withdraw their talents or equipment and force you to pay back the money they loaned. This weakens your position and efficiency. Sometimes they do not say that the things they give you to use are just being lent, and give you the impression that because of their "good heart" they want you to enjoy them. But with such a technique, they try to make you follow their instructions or directions, and if you are alert enough not to fall further into the trap, they present you with a bill for the articles you used and are still using — a bill that you are forced to pay whether you like it or not because, first of all, you used the equipment and, secondly, you do not want to "make it a court case."

A man once came to a leader and gave him a nice piano, which the leader received gratefully. Because the leader was given this piano, he sold his old one for a cheap price. After one year, the person asked for the return of the piano, or eight thousand dollars in fifteen days. Because of the work the leader was doing on the piano, he was forced to borrow money from the bank for the piano. Additionally, he lost money on the sale of his old piano, which would have been fine for his work. He also was placed in the position of paying back a large loan, with interest.

The Ageless Wisdom says not to take anything for free, not to take anything with strings attached, not to take things you already have.

If these rules are obeyed, many headaches can be avoided on the path of leadership.

35

A Few Practical Steps for Leaders

A leader must see to it that he has able people around him. If he has sick or depressed people around him, people who are involved in their own problems, people who are full of gossip, slander, treason, or jealousy, he cannot do his job and he fails because of

    a. His wrong choice

    b. The absence of able people

    c. His own weaknesses

The weaknesses of a leader need further explanation:

1. He is not daring and courageous enough to change his co-workers.

2. He has vices about which his co-workers know.

3. He has secrets which are known by his co-workers.

4. He has attachment to co-workers.

5. He does not closely check all that his co-workers are doing.

6. He does not have direct communication with his co-workers and does not hold frequent meetings with them to talk face to face.

Such weaknesses make him a weak leader.

A real leader must try to help his co-workers immediately upon seeing that they are in trouble. He must not let their mistakes grow and become irreparable, unless he wants to give them "more rope to hang themselves."

A leader must watch over the state of their ego, vanity, or showing off and should lose no time in making his co-workers confront themselves. If he tolerates mistakes, he cannot have good co-workers. It is also important to know the cause of the mistakes so that he does not blame his co-workers unrighteously.

If after disciplinary action the leader discovers that he was mistaken in his judgment, he must not hesitate to ask for forgiveness from his co-workers. Sincerity and humility are great signs of leadership.

How do we make our co-workers more able and efficient? Here are seven steps:

1. See if they fit the job. If they do, then train them for the job they are to do and have them practice frequently.

2. Watch to see if they are interested in improving how they do their job by trying to learn more.

3. Try to find the sources of their weaknesses, if there are any.

4. See if they can cooperate with other co-workers.

5. See if they know how, when, and what to speak, and when to keep silent.

6. See if they follow your instructions in detail.

7. See if they have solemnity.

With these seven observations you can stand guard, and take the necessary action, and it will be difficult for the co-workers to take advantage of you.

If you see that someone must be removed, be righteous and do not delay his removal. Take fast action. All such actions must be taken with nobility and with loving understanding.

How can we produce able people? Able people do not pop up like popcorn. You must find them, train them, prepare them, and then give them a method with which they can improve themselves.

Not everyone can be a leader. They must really want it and dedicate themselves to it with all their heart and sincerity.

How can we find a leader? Look for the following qualities:

1. Healthy

2. Persevering in learning and practice

3. Disciplined

4. Free from habits

5. Observant and awake

6. Fearless

7. Solemn

8. Sacrificial

9. Humble

You can add many other characteristics, but the ones given above are clear indications of leadership.

How can we train our leaders?

We can train people to become leaders by making them

    a. Meditate

    b. Study

    c. Serve

How can we prepare our leaders?

    1. Give them duties.

    2. Give them responsibilities.

    3. Closely watch them.

Every night they must sit quietly and reflect on the labor of the day, checking their work, their speech, their relationships and thinking. Then they can correct or improve themselves in their mind and decide to improve the situation the next day.

One can be a great leader by following these methods in detail for thirty minutes daily.

It is advisable that any leader-to-be informs his leader directly of any short-comings. The leader must not try to argue with him or convince him of his failures. The leader can show him briefly that his action was not beautiful, good, righteous, joyful, goal-fitting, or based on "free judgment." This means judgment that is free from of self-interests, vanity, ego, glamor, and illusion and is not conditioned by them.

    Arguments imprint a co-worker with his weaknesses, and he will try to cover them. When you start digging into the past failures of your co-worker, into his bad intentions, lack of obedience, and so on, you make him identify with his *not-self*, but your intention is to help him detach from his lower or not-self. You must remove a co-worker from his duties and make him take a vacation, if necessary.

If he becomes eager to meet the standards and return to work, be very cautious and keep him under your observation. Sometimes the person returns to cause complications.

To improve your co-workers, you must not try to act as their policeman or judge. Whenever you turn into a policeman or a judge, you lose the game. On the contrary, you must give them standards and make them become their own policeman and judge.

If they are successful in seeing their deficiencies, help them improve without criticizing them. When you catch them in their failure, ask them why they did it and then wait for the answer.

An honest man will not blame others for his mistake. He will be the first to accept his mistake and then measure it against the standards you have given to him. He will also point out exactly why he made the mistake.

Any sign of self-justification or rationalization indicates to you that you are dealing with a dangerous person, and you must not engage in any argument with him. A sincere and honest co-worker will immediately try to take action to correct his mistakes, even with sacrificial service.

The important points in this instruction can be formulated as follows. Do not deal with or discuss the causes of the mistake with your co-worker. Deal only with the mistake and the correction of the mistake. The leader himself must determine the causes. When you deal with the causes of the mistake with the one who made the mistake, you are dealing with dangerous material, such as:

— Wrong motives

— Inner and outer problems

— Karmic defects

— Bad intentions

These are the things that the person making the mistake always wants to hide. Trying to make the person reveal these problems to you is almost a crime. But if the person reveals them to you, your reaction will be silent observation to see if he is covering up or is speaking the truth. In both cases, any comment from you will make him feel worse.

Insincere and self-interested "co-workers" hate to see their mistakes, and they find the ways and means to take your attention away from the mistake and focus it on the weather, on the relationships of others, on their health problems, and so on. They might even accuse you and your lack of attention to them.

You must not occupy yourself with this "dynamite" but emphasize again and again the work to be done and what the standards are.

The mistake itself will knock them down, not your judgment, analysis, or condemnation. Let the mistake itself judge them. Let the worker understand the existence of the mistake. Once this is done, he will not try to cover up because the mistake is evident. He can hide the causes but not the mistake. He can even justify himself . . . but not the mistake.

You must know that traitors are very skilled in confessing things that are not true. They like to condemn themselves and ask you to punish them. If you have no future hope for them, never try to punish them. They will use your punishment as a road back to you. One of the techniques I use is to ask them if they want to continue to stay in that position and make more mistakes. Usually they resign from their position, and often they vanish.

It is very important to have a file on each co-worker and note in that file, with the dates, the mistakes they made and their reactions or the wonderful things they did and your responses. Such a file can help you in making better future decisions.

A true leader is one who opens the sense of value in his co-workers, makes them see the beauty which is developing in others, and helps them learn how to recognize others and how to cooperate with them.

A true leader must not be separative in his leadership. He must not encourage his co-workers to think that apart from themselves, nothing exists.

It is pitiful to see that some leaders continually attack any new sprout, scared that a new sprout will cast a shadow upon them. Real leadership rejoices in every achievement because, for a real leader, every achievement belongs to him and every person who achieves is a part of himself.

Some people have a great devotion toward great Teachers, but, surprisingly, they reject or even hate those who strive toward greatness. This jealousy is so strong in some people that they even slander those who speak about the Great Ones, as if the Great Ones were their own property.

Great damage is done in rejecting or belittling those talents who manifest striving toward greatness. Leaders must continuously challenge, inspire, and encourage the little ones, just as a gardener so lovingly takes care of the sprouts, because from these little ones the future giants will be formed.

The duty of the leader is to search for and find true talents and give them the opportunity to prove themselves. Each constructive and creative work must be encouraged.

One of my teachers used to say that a true leader is like a collector of talents. He used to call talents "jewels." One day he showed us a chalice ornamented with fifteen different kinds of jewels. After words of admiration, he asked, "What do you think? Would this chalice be more beautiful if it had been decorated with only one kind or with one color of gem?" We all agreed that its beauty was based on the variety of the jewels that were arranged in such a harmonious way. "You are right," said the Teacher. "Every great and potent group is a collection of many talents, harmonized with each other around a purpose."

A leader is not a purpose, but he is a source of inspiration in the search for the purpose. A true leader collects the various talents to work for the purpose. Purpose can be understood better and served better by synchronizing the interpretation and labor of all talents.

LEADERSHIP GUIDELINES

Leadership is a different path. Here are some guidelines:

1. You need control of your mouth to know where to speak, what to speak, and how to approach problems and people with your speech.

2. You need endurance and patience. People and problems cannot be handled easily. The leader must approach them with the intention to win people and solve problems. The smallest victory over problem people and difficulties is a beginning for total victory. Sometimes a slow approach and a small victory can lead to a bigger victory than a fast approach victory.

Patience and endurance give you time to study problem people and difficulties from many angles and find the best approach.

As long as you are honest and your motives are right, do not worry about your victory. It will come in due time, during which your endurance and patience will be tempered.

3. You need to learn the tactics of withdrawal and attack. Sometimes a retreat brings more victory than an attack. Give time to problem people to see your viewpoint. Do not threaten them. You are not supposed to attack people but to solve their problems. When their problems are solved, they turn into co-workers.

4. Be careful of those who easily agree with you. Often the traitors come from these ranks. Question them as to why they agree with you. Is it because of fear, of self-interest, or for revenge on others? What makes them agree with you so easily?

Even if they are innocent, make them understand the causes or motives of your moves. Make them show you that they agree with you consciously.

5. Do not encourage your followers to sink into inertia. Inertia invites obsession, and sooner or later such people abandon the field of battle. Give them jobs to do, and see that they do them with enthusiasm and devotion. Remember, you need people to take your place and be efficient leaders.

6. Do not build them artificially by giving them plenty of advice and hoping that your advice will make them leaders. Leaders are prepared in labor and battle against hindering circumstances. Release them into the field, and watch them as they work. It is better to teach them in the field than in the classroom. Remember, Krishna gave the highest teaching on the battlefield.[1]

7. Do not let criticism and slander affect your work. You can learn many valuable lessons from criticism, but if it slows you down, discourages you, and weakens you, it means the one who is criticizing you is controlling you.

Learn from your mistakes. Try to correct them, and then forget the sources of criticism. Never react against them but, after a feeling of gratitude, forget them.

8. Try not to hurt people because of your wounds. A leader fails when he acts under the pain of his wounds.

Leadership is possible if one can withdraw his consciousness from the personality and focus it in the soul during leadership activities. A leader fails if he mixes his personality reactions with the guidance he gives to others.

Also, self-interest in guidance brings about the downfall of leadership. The more the personality-self is left out of the guidance, the more powerful will be the leadership.

Some false leaders misguide people as if they were enemies. These false leaders try to satisfy their hurt feelings, jealousy, or revenge.

9. Never exercise your leadership while in a depressed condition. Try to give your command when you feel strong or really joyful. It is in the light of joy that your guidance, direction, or command become charged with a special power. Guidance given in a depressed mood carries your personality influence to people and creates reactions from their lower self.

10. Learn that one of the important virtues a leader must develop can be called "recovery after being beaten" by

>Karma
>
>Slander
>
>Failure
>
>Errors made, etc.

Leadership must be a path of periodic recovery. A leader must know that every time he is beaten down a great opportunity is given to him to test his

>Efficiency
>
>Resourcefulness
>
>Energy level
>
>Selflessness
>
>Perseverance, etc.

He must not give up, knowing that "giving up" is the greatest failure. No defeat or failure is greater than giving up.

All difficulties must come and go, and the leader, like a Phoenix, must rise from the ashes of past experiences of failure and defeat.

The greatest invincible leaders are those who "stand up" after every attack or defeat.

FURTHER GUIDANCE FOR LEADERS

1. Solemnity appears in the aura as a tense field of energy which radiates peace, blessings, and uplifting colors to its surroundings.

This is true for the aura of a Temple, a group, or an individual.

For example, in a Temple, you have an aura that is stable, tense, peaceful, inspiring, uplifting, and enlightening. Solemnity is like a divine presence dominating there.

The sphere of solemnity is affected by noise, loud speech, silly jokes, ugly expressions, the clapping of hands, or jerky movements. This is true in a personal sense as well as in relation to the group or Temple aura.

The shattering of the aura can continue and will slowly lead to degeneration when, through jerky movements and hand clapping, people induce various kinds of emotions into the aura.

It is not easy to keep the aura of solemnity stable because of various habits of speech, action, and changing mood. But those who can keep the solemnity long enough, their whole aura turns into a magnet which attracts higher impressions from Space, bringing them not only wisdom but also power.

The solemnity and dignity of the Temple or Ashram must be kept by all means.

One of the other things that destroys the aura is *cursing* charged with hatred and malice. Also, sexual acts or lust can destroy the aura of solemnity in sacred places.

Of course, karma hits those who introduce such pollutions.

2. One of the duties of the leader is to watch closely the work that the co-workers are doing in the various branches of the work. By closely watching them, he will see where they need help to be more efficient in their job and to develop their potentials which will help them in the future to be great leaders.

An uninterested leader, who is occupied with his work and problems, slowly lets everything disintegrate around him. When co-workers are not challenged, trained, and progressively made more efficient in their job, they are the ones who create the worst problems for the leader and for the work.

Each man of position must be closely watched. He must be inspired, challenged, even corrected, and moved if he is not in the right line of work. There are many kinds of workers:

— Those who waste time

— Those who waste materials

— Those who do not perform their duties and responsibilities

— Those who do not cooperate with the parts of the whole mechanism

— Those who slander

— Those who have fallen into malice and treason

— Those who pursue their own interests and work for their own vanity

— Those who distort the command or the plan of the leader

— Those who mislead their committee members

— Those who do not follow the training required of them

The leader must watch all these points and others more subtly related to their spiritual development. He must not be late in approaching and giving them right guidance. Negligence in his responsibility brings disaster to the life of a leader.

3. To give correct guidance a leader must have the right training in every part of the work. He must even have a few co-workers who can guide him in certain technical areas in which he

is not an expert. They can help him locate those activities which need improvement, change, or cancellation.

4. A good leader must have a check list for his co-workers and occasionally check them.

Some leaders do not do such a job for various reasons:

    a. They do not have a detached attitude.

    b. They are under the control of their subordinates because

    — of personal involvement with them

    — their subordinates know their weaknesses and shortcomings

    — for various reasons they are afraid to use pressure to correct their subordinates

    — they are faint-hearted

    — their spirit is not involved in the purpose of their work

A careless leader lets weeds increase to such a degree that they completely cover the paths of his work and present a hard barrier for his future pilgrims.

Every mistake must be corrected at the right time and without delay. And all opportunities must be presented to co-workers to be more efficient and cooperative in their fields.

5. A leader must know that co-workers who are in high positions are not necessarily the ones who can meet their duties and responsibilities with greater efficiency. He must know that there are those who work in lower levels, silently and humbly, who are more capable of doing better things than those in higher positions. A leader must search for such people, know them, and promote them to higher positions.

A leader's intention is to make the organization really efficient by introducing new promotions. His duty is to cultivate talents and put them in positions where they can bring much fruit.

In some organizations, people in higher positions stay there for many, many years, even if they do not produce the work expected of them.

A leader must wisely move his co-workers to different positions to bring the utmost out of them and to give others a chance to cultivate new capabilities. Thus the whole organization progresses toward a higher future efficiency.

When a talent is not cultivated and opportunities are not given to leaders-to-be, they slowly become dormant and fall into inertia, or they use their talents in destructive activities.

Recognition of talents and their promotion are two of the most noble duties of a leader.

There are some leaders who want to do the entire job by themselves. This is the path which leads to self-defeat. The leader's intention will be to prepare those who will pass him in leadership qualities and do things in the future that he was not capable of doing.

No one alone can actualize his vision. The actualization of a vision takes years and ages and always demands future leaders to carry the torch on and on.

If the work of a leader disintegrates after he passes away, this means he did not entrust his vision to the right, capable, efficient, and noble hands.

6. The actualization of the vision is more important than some limited work done for the vision. Every leader must fix his focus on the vision and not let his temporary work for the vision satisfy him.

Once a leader told his soldiers, "That is the peak which must be conquered. If I fall on the way, one of you must carry the work toward the summit. Even if the majority of you die on the path and just one reaches the summit, I will consider that success the achievement of the leadership."

Any work done on the path toward the summit has, of course, tremendous importance, but the goal is to reach the summit.

A true leader must organize the work in such a way that many of his co-workers will be able to replace him in various fields of duty and responsibility.

7. Young leaders must not only follow the discipline of the Elders in finding and promoting talents, but also they must ask their advice. The younger leaders must benefit from the experiences of the Elder leaders. Much confusion, loss of time, energy, and money can be spared by listening to the advice of an elder leader. This does not mean that young leaders are going to hang on to an elder leader, but they must use the opportunity to benefit from his wisdom.

It would be very beneficial if young leaders collected various leadership questions and problems and presented them to an elder leader to seek his guidance.

The overall effort is to make the vision actualized. It is not to search for personal qualifications, for opportunities to show off, or for prestige. Young leaders must be trained to be humble and not arrogant, so that they do not work because of personal pride and are not always seeking help from there Elders in the time of necessity.

They must always think, "What can we do to succeed in reaching the vision?" If self-renunciation is necessary, it must be done.

Many obstacles exist in the heart of those young leaders who avoid getting counselling from their Elders in cases of emergency or need. Of course, an elder leader must encourage young leaders not to depend on him but to go ahead with confidence and alertness. Even he will allow them to make mistakes to learn the mechanism of failure, but he will guide them based on his experience and wisdom and not let them fall into serious or fatal mistakes.

A close friendship must exist between elder leaders and young ones, and the elder leaders must always give an opportunity to young ones to participate in the labors and make them observe the Elders in various conditions and in various labors.

Besides technical advice, young leaders must seek out Elders to give them courage in difficult times of life, especially when passing through various kinds of pressures, failures, sicknesses, and suffering. The young ones must ask the advice of elder leaders and learn the ways they have used to overcome obstacles, slander, treason, and various kinds of attacks.

Some young leaders can be very efficient in technical duties, but they lack the fortitude to stand against many kinds of attacks. Much can be learned from elder leaders and put to use in times of emergency.

Again, of course, an elder leader must not try to solve the problems of young leaders but give them courage, inspire fearlessness, and daring, remove the hindrances from their consciousness, and release them into the field of battle.

Young leaders must not pretend that they are great leaders. Humility must be their guiding light. They must be trained in such a way that they are able to see themselves in operation with a detached attitude and immediately take action to improve themselves when their observation of their work does not fully satisfy the standards built in them.

Elder leaders must train young ones how to increase their faith, hope, and trust; how to see in a stormy sea the light of the beacon; how to sustain equilibrium when all around is unstable and moving; how to face the "enemy" built by past karma and use the karma to help push the wheel of their progress.

The success of the leader is the amount of transformation he brings into the lives of his co-workers. This success is not limited to individual transformation. It must be related to Cosmic Evolution. Each progress, success, or transformation must be based upon the concept of Cosmic Evolution. Your success is equal to the measure of advancement you introduced into one process of Cosmic Evolution.

Leaders must have this idea in front of each of their labors. The labor is done not for a person, not for a group, but to assist Cosmic Evolution. Such an attitude purifies the path of service and guarantees success. Those who work for Cosmic Evolution will never fail.

Service must be done in true faith that nothing is lost in the Universe and that all our labors are registered and have their effects. Such a faith slowly turns into an enthusiasm when the server starts to realize that the vision of Cosmic Evolution is conducting the orchestra of all his actions, feelings, thoughts, and creative expressions.

Thus the server does not work for this or that person, for this or that interest, group, or nation; for this or that tradition or religion; but he works only for the advancement of Cosmic Evolution. The vision of Cosmic Evolution turns into energy in all his activities, and nothing can discourage him; on the contrary, the limitations on the path multiply his efforts.

The real server is not interested in the visible and immediate forms of success. He knows that seeds thrown in space will bloom in the fields of Infinity, and the Cosmic Computer will not fail to record every seed thrown into space and every flower unfolding in space.

One of my Teachers, speaking one night near a bonfire, said, "One day, when true Servers visit higher realms, they will be surprised at seeing the gardens they were cultivating while on earth. They will notice that the best flowers in their gardens were nourished by their heavy sweat and tears while laboring on earth."

The day you commit yourself to serve Cosmic Evolution, a garden is given to you in space. Great Ones occasionally visit your garden to see it. Some gardens produce weeds; some produce a few flowers; others give the full beauty of many kinds of flowers. The latter kind of garden stays on higher planes, and life after life the server tries to cultivate it. If the garden is full of blooms, the angels enjoy it and make it a place of song, music, and dances. What a great vision to have such an idea in every effort of our labor!

Cosmic Evolution is going on within the Infinite Space. Only those who are free of self-interest can participate in this great labor. Commitment to the Great Cause and a firm decision to go ahead in the field of labor evoke the assisting forces of the Universe.

Every decision or determination in harmony with the currents of evolution creates a substance in the aura which attracts the energy of the Cosmic Magnet. It is this combination of energy and substance that gradually evokes and sustains the power in man which we call *will*.

It is also true that decisive actions taken against the currents of evolution evoke a response from the Cosmic Magnet, but the response is not used for the General Good and it is wasted in self-interest. This creates a heavy karmic debt for the subject. In this case, the power of the will is not conceived and developed.

The development of the will requires the element produced by right action and the response of the Cosmic Magnet.

Notes:

1. *Bhagavad Gita*, translated by author.

36
Rules for Telephone Conversations

It is impossible to tell you what to talk about specifically on the telephone, but the following points may help:

1. Professionalism is needed. You must keep your conversation restricted to business. This is good for business.

2. Keep your conversations short and to the point.

3. Do not answer questions which are not in your domain.

4. Do not give any health advice. Do not name any herb, oil, or medicine.

5. Do not counsel people on the telephone. If they need counseling, they can see a professional.

6. You can say a few encouraging words and suggest a few pages from the Teaching.

7. Personal stories and personal or family complaints must not be heard or talked about. If the speaker on the other end wants to continue to speak about his endless troubles, you can give the number of certain hotlines to help him or direct him to an organization dealing with certain difficulties.

8. If the person asks, "What is your group all about?" Say, "We will send you all the information if you give us your address."

9. If the person asks, "What do you teach?" Say, "We teach about Beauty, Goodness, Righteousness, Joy, and Freedom," or what briefly fits your organization. "If you would like more information, please give me your name and address."

10. To handle gossip, say, "I am not the person to hear your gossip. Address yourself to the one you are gossiping about. We do not act as intermediaries."

11. You can make excuses to cut a conversation short: "I am sorry, but I have to leave . . . . I have work to do . . . . A visitor is here . . . . I am in conference," etc.

12. If people ask about classes or directions to the office, be clear, short, professional, and kind.

13. If they ask about the books or products, you may read from the descriptions in the brochure.

14. If they ask about the leader of the group, briefly state that he is a writer, a speaker, etc., and you can see him by appointment. Take the person's name, address, telephone number, his profession, and the reason he wants to see the leader.

15. Unless absolutely necessary, keep the telephone lines free for emergencies or important calls.

16. Business lines should not be busy more than two to three minutes maximum.

17. Personal, "passing time" conversations are not tolerated. Only emergency personal calls are allowed. Long distance calls are not authorized.

Collect calls will NOT be accepted *unless* prior arrangements have been made.

18. If anyone, besides the employees, wants to use the telephone:

    a. be sure it is an emergency

    b. be sure to listen to what he says and what number he is dialing

    c. interfere if necessary

19. It is strictly forbidden to speak about politics or legal affairs on the telephone.

20. Keep in mind why we are here and Who we are really working for.

21. Read these rules often to assimilate them.

22. The leader may check your line to see if you are obeying the rules.

GUIDELINES FOR TELEPHONE CONVERSATIONS

1. When you ask a question, wait until the person gives you an answer.

2. If you are not satisfied, ask a question again and wait.

3. Do not try to give answers to your own questions, and do not change the topic until you are satisfied.

4. Do not ask many questions at once. This is confusing for you and for the person at the other end.

5. Do not tell him about the answers people gave previously to the same question.

6. Do not try to *help* him answer your question.

7. Do not put questions in the mouth of the caller.

8. Make your conversations clear, simple, sincere, and professional, which means talk about things that are within the limit of your subject.

9. In official calls, do not discuss personal problems and stories. Do not criticize or flatter or attack. Use your best logic and reasoning.

10. Some people show excitement on the telephone. It is better to be warm, joyful, but not driven by the winds of emotions, exclamations, etc.

11. In your personal conversations be careful, knowing that the other end can tape all you are saying and use it against you.

12. Do not talk in a way that creates suspicion on any subject. Clarity is the key in conversation.

13. Do not talk about the private life of someone on your telephone — neither about your secrets or the secrets of others. Know that you may have more than one listener.

14. Speak only within the borderlines of your position. Neither give commands nor answer questions if they are not your business. You most probably will do wrong talking about the office or the responsibility of another person.

15. Try never to advise about personal or family health problems. Instead, suggest they see a specialist. An advice can be used against you.

16. Do not give out addresses or telephone numbers of your co-workers to any strange persons. They may have wrong motives in their minds.

17. When you are talking to government officials, you must be very accurate. You must understand clearly what they want and who is in the office who can give the accurate answer.

18. Try never to give a wrong answer.

19. If a person wants to chat on the telephone, do not create an argument. Instead, say, I cannot stay on the line so long or, ask questions one after the other:

— your name

— occupation

— beliefs

— books you read

— faith

— do you read our books

— what do you want to accomplish in your life?

Please know that after you ask your questions you must only listen.

If the person is on long distance, he will quit. If the person asks your name, don't deal with personality requests.

20. If the person asks you what is the opinion of another person in the group, you should refer the caller to that person. Do not be a spokesman for another person.

21. Answer your calls with a clear, joyful, and positive voice. Never show fear, depression, or anger. Stay calm. Some people answer telephone calls as if they were sick or frustrated or in a hurry, or as if the food on the stove were burning.

37

Studying Both Sides

We can obtain a better balance in our judgment, relationships, and evaluations when our consciousness is capable of studying both sides of a problem or the two extremes of any object.

For example, those who are materialists and are occupied only with the labor of accumulating money and possessions, or with business, banking, and so on, are not dependable persons as far as their judgment on world problems is concerned.

Also, those who are dedicated to abstract values and objects and who are occupied exclusively with transcendental values are not dependable persons as far as their judgment is concerned. Their viewpoint is limited by abstract values, and they do not have balance in their judgment. Such people are walking in the air.

The people who will have better judgment, better relationships, and a more acceptable life are those who can balance both extremes and find the path that solves any problem without disregarding either the material or the abstract values. Abstract values cannot be useful without the existence of material values, and material values cannot be useful for people except when they are balanced by abstract values. Abstract values are just as important as material values; the two must coexist in our judgment if our judgment is going to be sound.

We can look at this subject from another angle. We may say that material values are the effect of spiritually caused values or that spiritual values are the effect of materially caused values. From whatever angle we approach this problem, one thing can be seen: both extremes are related, and sound judgment is the approximation of both extremes.

Once my Teacher wanted to help me to see what would happen if I did and did not do certain things. He gave me five things to do and not to do. One was, "What could happen if you learned something new every day for ten years, for one hundred years, for two thousand years? Then what would happen if you did not learn anything new for ten years, one hundred years, or two thousand years?" I would be occupied answering such questions for months. This exercise took me from zero to the greatest extreme I could imagine. The effect was miraculous. After I began to see both extremes, my judgment and relationships became more balanced; they were *goal-fitting*.

I remember one day for some fun I filled a trench with water and covered it with straw and dry grass to see if some careless boy would fall into it. All of those who fell in were very angry, but some joined me in the game when they saw the possibility of another boy's fall. Five boys were trapped; two went and complained. The Teacher wanted to know who did it, but he said, "I know it is embarrassing to reveal the truth, but I will give you one day to confess — and punishment will not be easy."

That day and night I used the instruction of my other Teacher to see both ends, both extremes of the situation. I contemplated that

1. It would be a defeat to my soul if I lied.
2. If the truth was later discovered, it would be more humiliating.

3. If they did not find out, it would be a wound in my soul.

4. I would lose the friendship of my Teacher, psychologically avoiding him because of my guilt.

5. I might disturb my conscience and create a cleavage between my soul and the Angel.

On the other hand, if I confessed

1. I would prove that I was honest and brave.

2. The punishment would not be too severe because of my honesty and innocent nature.

3. I might not get fed for a few days.

4. But everyone would love me because of my courage.

After reviewing again and again both extremes, I decided to confess. So I went to the Dean's office the next morning with a big smile on my face and said, "I guess you know it was me!" He pretended he was busy with some book, and in a very loving voice, said, "Think about what would happen if a boy cut his leg or hurt himself."

"Yes, sir."

"The case is closed."

I left his office in silence, with mixed feelings. I almost wanted him to say a few harsh words to me. On the other hand, I was proud of myself but also humiliated by creating such a stupid game to trap people. But how noble my Teacher was. He did not hurt my feelings, scold me, or give me a lecture.

From that date on I behaved with more solemnity. When it was time for me to leave the monastery, the Dean hugged me and whispered in my ear. "Every victory is achieved through internal conflict. Always try to be the victor in that battle." My mind often finds the right solution to a problem by evaluating both extremes.

Life is a dance performed between two extremes.

38

Leadership and Co-Workers

The leader or the leadership must know the character of his co-workers and see their motives and intentions so that

1. He leads them into the right positions
2. He helps them overcome the defective sides of their character
3. He helps them to develop right motives
4. He protects them in such a way that they do not hurt themselves and/or the group

A leader cannot operate efficiently unless he has the power to see the character and motives of the people around him. To obtain this information, he needs time and he has to create crises and then watch. It is in crises that the true character and true motives of people around him surface.

The leader must not depend only on his own intuition and past experience, but also he must draw on his factual and realistic observations.

People are often very clever in the way they hide their motives and the leader sometimes must wait a long time to reach a realistic conclusion. It is even recommended that, in order to see the defective sides of his co-workers, the leader wait until "the mouse is completely out of his hole" and can no longer hide himself.

The leader must decide how long he is going to wait because sometimes a wrongly-motivated person can execute fatal damage during the period in which the leader is waiting for him to come "out of his hole."

There is another tactic which the leader must use in his sacrificial service. On some occasions he must retreat, but on other occasions he must "attack." In retreat he must observe the activities of his co-workers, and then "attack" them when he sees that they are going in the wrong direction.

He can even wait so that those who are going in the wrong direction are well involved in their wrong doings. This is sometimes very helpful in the sense that the failing ones have no chance to justify themselves.

The overall motive of the leader or the leadership must be to strengthen the co-workers and prepare them in such a way that they will be able in the future to take heavier responsibilities on their shoulders.

Those who show signs of leadership must be trained systematically through practical means. They must not only have good character and right motive, but they must also have skills in how not to be defeated by those who will try to trap them and use them against their own motives or intentions. Also they must have experience in how to protect their co-workers from various attacks.

Some co-workers wait to see obvious signs of treason before taking action, but real leadership does not wait until the organism is decayed. It watches carefully for the first sign of sickness to prevent it from spreading further.

Every leader must learn how to see the first signs of character defects and erosion of motives.

Co-workers must be educated to think more about the flow of labor than about their role in the labor.

To explain the above, we may say that co-workers sometimes attach to the work they are doing or have done and feel emotional if someone else continues their job, corrects it, improves it, or makes it more up to date. Under such conditions many emotions play out, creating difficulties and complications among the group of co-workers.

An experienced co-worker must not fall into any such trap because his concern must not be his role in the job but in the evolution of the job. He must encourage, invite, and have conferences with those who can share the labor and make it more fruitful and productive. Instead, some co-workers hate the job they were doing when it is taken from their hands and given to someone else who can do it better or even fill a gap in the job.

The important issue in the mind of a co-worker must be how to make a certain job perfect, or how to improve it steadily without creating an imbalance in other labors going on which are related to that job.

If a co-worker insists that only he should do the job, or if he demonstrates uneasiness or irritation when a job is taken away from him and given to another, then he proves that a mistake was made in choosing him for the job in the first place.

The flow of work must be continuous. Co-workers must understand that their primary duty is to guarantee the flow of work and to improve the work. Personal issues are secondary matters; the job is the most essential issue.

Co-workers, by any means possible, must learn to have a detached attitude in their dedication to the labor. Any attachment to any part of the labor indicates that the co-worker is laboring for his self-interest, ego, and vanity.

One day my Teacher, showing the flow of a river, said, "Look how interesting it is. The ripples in the river are co-workers. But the flow of the river is the job, the work which must continue steadily, in spite of the ripples which are blown against or on the current."

This was a seed thought of meditation for me. And many things were revealed to me during this meditation.

The work must go on with our labor, with the labor of all co-workers in this life, life after life, unceasingly. And we must be increasingly ready to contribute to the work with greater efficiency.

In certain circumstances a leader learns to sacrifice his co-workers and his beloved ones for a great cause or for their own benefit, at the expense of the work he is doing. At certain times it is better to release a co-worker

1. To protect the work from his karmic developments

2. To help him to work out his problems

3. To protect other co-workers from karmic contamination

For the leader this is a sacrifice, first, because the co-worker will leave a vacuum behind which needs to be filled as soon as possible if there are people who can meet the requirements. Second, the released one may present problems for the group while he is struggling with his karma.

For the leader, personal interests and personal relations must be sacrificed for the benefit of the person and for the benefit of the group. A conscious co-worker must resign himself from the group if he begins to pass through periods of crisis which in any way affect the group. This will be a great help for the leader because it will eliminate the burden of many anxieties from his shoulders.

If a dismissed co-worker wants to solve his karmic problems sooner and more intelligently, he will keep esoteric silence and even vanish for a while, until the karmic turbulences are settled, in order not to involve the group in his complications. The dismissed one or the resigned one can be a door of attack for dark forces. This is why the leader and co-workers must exercise extreme caution in handling him or relating to him.

The dark ones often delay their attacks until a good opportunity is given to them by the victim. The best opportunity is the period of time in which karma is intensely active and the victim is unaware of it, or when he has lost control over the karmic waves. This is why a leader must always develop a detached attitude toward his co-workers and be ready to sacrifice them in spite of his personal concerns, ties, and friendship.

If a dismissed co-worker solves his problems intelligently and is released from his karmic ties, the leader must not reinstall him in his former duties. First he must watch the co-worker for a period of two years to see if the emotions and thoughts are stabilized and the motive to serve shines in its purity. Even after the leader is convinced of his safety, the co-worker must not be put in responsible positions for one year.

Some people show cooperation in order to take lots of responsibilities on their shoulders; not with the intention of helping you but of gaining power over you and making their increasing demands to be met. They do this because they think, "The leader will collapse if I withdraw all my engagements and responsibilities." The leader must be very careful not to depend on one person for many works and always give the duties to two or three persons so that he does not fall under anyone's control.

39

The Center and the Circle

When leadership is discussed, many people think only about themselves individually and their need to know how to become a real leader. This is an important part of leadership, but it is not complete.

Without a circle there will be no center. The center is the leader. The most important labor is to create the circle. What is the circle? The circle is formed by those who are sensitive to the Plan and Purpose presented to them through the center.

After such sensitive souls are attracted to the center, the responsibility of the center is to educate, discipline, and cultivate in them various skills through which they will be able to express the direction and the Plan coming through the center.

If the center needs scientific, artistic, or financial people or people who can meet various demands of the center, he will send a call into the subjective planes. Sensitive souls, ready to develop their skills, will emerge, and the circle of expression or manifestation will be formed.

The center will simultaneously express the Plan and Purpose through the individuals forming the circle.

After a very close affinity is established between the center and the personnel of the circle, the duty of the center will be to draw the circle to the center and make them a nucleus of a future circle.

The previous center will be released for more responsible services.

When we say the "center," people understand it as a person. But the right translation of the word will show us that the center is a mechanism — or a collective mechanism — which is able to focus a part of the Plan and transmit the lightning of the Purpose.

The center is not a personality but a Spiritual Triad. Every Spiritual Triad is composed of four entities. Each angle of the Triad is a Nirvani, and at the center is the human soul. Thus the center is essentially a group represented in form by one or more individualities.

No center can be guaranteed success even if the leader is a high degree initiate. His success depends on four factors:

1. The quality of those who form his circle — their readiness, their skill, their purity, their dedication, and their ability to understand the "command."

2. The time factor. His labor must fall within the timetable of the Plan.

3. The ability of the center to keep the right distance from the circumference. Do not forget that the center uses the Law of Attraction or Repulsion.

4. Sensitivity to timing — when the center will draw the circle into the center and be released to do greater work wherever he is needed.

Most leaders work upon themselves, but real leaders offer equal time to prepare co-workers. The preparation of co-workers is as essential as the graduation into leadership. The leader must have specialists working as a group to translate adequately the streams of inspirations and impressions coming from the Core.

The evolution of a leader is similar to the evolution of a human soul. The human soul advances by preparing more sensitive and complete vehicles. Then he tries to integrate these vehicles into one mechanism. Then he fuses with them. Then he withdraws into the Triad, into complete leadership of the lives which composed his vehicles.

Then the spiritualization of the vehicles accumulates, and the vehicles advance into leadership positions.

This is how nature works toward Infinity. Every emancipated or resurrected center cyclically sacrifices itself and serves those who served him as circumferences, as mechanisms for his service and manifestation.

CONTINUITY

One of the characteristics of the true leader is that he shows respect to the preceding leaders and never in any way belittles them, blames them, curses them, or tries to find errors in their conduct. Every true leader is the embodiment of his group. In insulting a leader we insult the group and create confusion and cleavages in it.

Every true leader, even after he leaves his body, does not cease thinking about the group he led and about the future the group may have.

To let the leader proceed on his path of perfection means not to speak about him in a humiliating way but, on the contrary, to remember him with gratitude and respect. It means to try to fulfill his constructive plans which he desired to bring into actualization but could not because the time was too short. It is very good to mention his various achievements and services and to quote his challenging words and his wisdom. Leaders must not consider themselves as individuals but as part of a chain of individuals formed of those who went before him and those who will come after him.

Belittling any leader for selfish ends or for personal considerations creates a very bad taste in the public consciousness. At the same time, people responsible for group work must not allow negative, destructive, or humiliating conduct on the part of any leader.

The true leaders of the past, present, and future must link with each other and carry the torch, which has been put into their hands, with more dedication and sacrificial service. A leader knocks down his own work by insulting his predecessors. On the other hand, he succeeds in his labor by revealing many beautiful events from the life of the previous leaders and by trying to make people know that the previous leaders did their best in the given conditions and gave him the torch to be carried further.

I remember once when a new leader was elected in the monastery because of the death of the former one. The new leader's first address was all about the previous leader. He said, "He was my teacher, my example, and a man of extreme courage, righteousness, and wisdom." He ended his speech by saying, "I pray that his spirit helps me in this difficult position. I will follow his steps and his principles in order to be worthy for him."

I remember that his term in office as leader was short. He took office when he was seventy-five and passed away at eighty-five. In all his conversations he used to mention the previous leader as a great and sacrificial man who was "enlightened from above."

Continuity is a mysterious principle. People must feel that there is continuity in speech, in teaching, in love. Whenever a link is broken by a word or attitude, it creates a wound in the body of the group.

Such an attitude of respect toward leaders must be cultivated in the hearts of followers. Followers, students, and those who search must see magnanimity in their leaders. Only pseudo leaders knock down the preceding ones to gain attention; but their behavior turns against them, and they lose the respect of those who cooperate with them.

LONELINESS

After every ascent there comes a time of loneliness. The life of the disciple has three phases:

    a. Aspiration, striving, labor

    b. Joy of achievement, radiation, success

c. Loneliness

This is a spiral path, which repeats itself on higher and higher spirals.

The first phase is full of friction, battle, pain, suffering, and conflict in which the spirit is tempered, the richness of the Inner Core is evoked, and the path of success is discovered.

In the second phase, the co-workers are attracted, the need is met, a higher level of consciousness is attained. In this stage, the soul radiates his beauty and enjoys the blessings pouring out from his and others' hearts.

In the third phase, a new vision is seen, a vision which puts him under a new discipline to concentrate and focus his time, energy, consciousness, and heart to actualize that vision and to assimilate the energies contacted through his achievement. Here begins a short or long period of loneliness.

In loneliness you collect into your heart the essence, the wisdom, of your past achievements, and you prepare yourself for a more difficult journey toward higher achievements. It is only this phase of loneliness that will give you power to transcend yourself and make yourself ready for future, more challenging services. But often, when this third phase comes, people slide back to the second phase or even the first phase, and instead of going forward, they repeat the path which they have already trodden.

Discipleship is a steady progress toward higher achievements in order to serve in a greater capacity and in higher positions. This is why the disciple must learn to detach from past achievements, past values, past pleasures, and past objects. This detachment is *tested*, *proved*, and *actualized* only during the phase of loneliness in which the human soul completely cuts himself from his past image and strives for a new and higher image.

The most precious years of our lives are the years in which we are alone but occupied with a striving to conquer, to create, and to achieve. All great objects of art, all great discoveries, all great plans and heroic deeds are conceived and created in loneliness.

It is in loneliness that your true nature finds the freedom to express its glory.

40

Lecturing

Leaders and lecturers must use a language that is acceptable and normal for the audience. This is why one must know well the kind of audience he is talking to.

It is easier to convey a message that is given through familiar words or expressions. People must accept you before they accept your instruction. The best way to do this is to create an affinity between the teacher and the audience. Using familiar words, parables, or expressions helps the audience accept the speaker. After the audience accepts the teacher, it accepts the instruction because the instruction is given through words and expressions which do not create a reaction in the audience.

Some teachers use a sophisticated language totally foreign to the audience, and the audience rejects things which it does not understand. After five minutes, the mind of the audience wanders in various places.

Each word for people is not a mere word but a chain of meanings. Such wealth can be used by the speaker to reach people easily and convey abundant meanings, whereas a forced expression create repulsion.

If you are lecturing to people in a specialized field, you must know their language to reach them. This is why the speaker must know many "languages" and use a specific one where it is necessary.

Once a woman came and spoke about her husband being an agnostic or an unbeliever. She said, "For ten years I am talking to him about consciousness. He rejects me. He is an electrical engineer."

It happened that one day we met. He enjoyed talking to me about electricity and about the work that electricity does for humanity and for the future of humanity. He liked me very much because I listened to him very carefully, asked questions, and made him explain deeper parts of the science. A few times I even asked him to explain a few terms which were not clear to me.

After two hours of conversation he suddenly said, "Electricity operates very mysteriously. Don't you think so?"

"Yes, yes," I said. "It seems to me that it operates as the consciousness does."

He looked at me and said, "Let us eat." At the table he was mentally preoccupied or absent.

Three weeks later he called and said, "Now I understand what the consciousness is. I didn't want to talk with my wife about it because *she was not accepting my knowledge* and not talking in my language."

This is why it is important to listen and to answer in the same language. Speech is as important as listening.

A Great Sage says, "We propose to adopt the language of the listener in all its characteristics."[1]

The speaker must also be able to relate himself to different characteristics of different races and nationalities. Even if he cannot use the words of their language, he should speak their psychological language and create affinity with them.

This is why before a lecturer speaks in a foreign country, it will be very profitable for him and for his audience if he studies their history, legends, myths, religion, their freedom, and their aspirations.

He must talk their psychological language to be accepted by them. When one fails to speak people's psychological language or to understand their language, he creates gaps in his consciousness and gaps between him and his audience.

This is why the leader-to-be must be exposed to various kinds and levels of people to experience and learn as many "languages" as possible if he is interested in being a victorious server-leader.

Often people do not have difficulty understanding certain theories, philosophical concepts, and abstract ideas, but they have an intense difficulty relating these theories, concepts, and ideas to their everyday life. Sometimes it is very helpful to such people if the writer or speaker takes an everyday example, elaborates upon it, and leads people's minds to the foundations of such stories and events.

Every event and happening is either a flowering of an idea or principle or the degeneration of it.

It will be easy for people to climb toward an abstraction or vision if a ladder is provided for them. A ladder symbolizes an event which is grounded in the practical daily life but can lead us up and make us have a better view of our daily life and experiences. This is why, for example, Christ and Buddha used so many beautiful and simple parables. They tried to make these parables like ladders leading people toward certain hidden principles or laws.

So, try to tell meaningful stories and make them build in a way that each part of the story can be taken as a translation or interpretation of an abstract idea, vision, or principle. In doing this, you enlighten people's daily life by giving them tools to solve their problems and handle their life under the light of higher ideas, visions, and principles.

Once I read a beautiful parable from Buddhist literature which explained how everything in Nature is dependent on everything else. Shariputra, a disciple of Buddha, said, "Suppose there are two bundles of reeds. They can remain standing as long as they lean against each other. In like manner, because this exists, that exists, and again, because that exists, this exists. If one of the two bundles is removed, then the other will fall. Similarly, without this existence, that cannot exist, and without that existence, this cannot exist."

This little story can grow into a philosophical treatise, slowly expanding our consciousness in such a way that every word of it glows in our mind in its higher dimensions.

Another example comes from Christian literature: "If a seed of grain does not fall into the earth, it cannot multiply."

Meditation is the ability to see the abstract connections and implications of something very basic, earthy, and simple. Speech is the ability to explain to others, in simplicity, what you discovered in meditating on parables, events, etc.

When we develop seeing eyes we will be able to understand that every event is an expression of a cause — a thought, an action, a law, a principle, an idea. The responsibility of a speaker will be to show his audience those subtle threads which relate the event to the cause and to show the program of steps leading to the cause.

Understanding is nothing else but an act of seeing the cause or causes of events, or of seeing what the cause produced in our daily life experiences. Thus the speaker or writer builds bridges or ladders and lets people ascend from events to their causes, or descend from causes to events. In this way he establishes the field of understanding in their minds.

Certain people cannot build these bridges or ladders, thereby leading their audience or readers into confusion. Whoever creates confusion is eventually abandoned by people or rejected by them.

Strengthening ties with people is the cause of the growth and expansion of a speaker's or writer's influence. Likewise, every bridge or ladder builder strengthens the audience as well and nourishes it with the food of the higher spheres.

The practice eventually develops in the speaker or writer a talent for metaphorical speech. Metaphorical speech is multidimensional speech. It has many levels, and it simultaneously enlightens many levels of the human mind, or many rooms of the human being. When people are hit, or enlightened, in many departments of their being, they respect and love the one who was able to do it.

The secret of those literatures which live through the centuries and always regenerate themselves is that they hit various departments of a human being. As a man grows and penetrates many new spheres of his being, he finds out that he can still enjoy reading that book because it still illuminates the newly discovered spheres of his being.

But the question is, who can write such a book? — Only a person who is himself multidimensional. And how does such a person come into being? — Only through looking at events from many viewpoints and trying to think from the cause to the events and from the events to the cause.

ADDITIONAL GUIDELINES FOR LEADERS

1. Lecturers must not use the opportunity to attack people, try and correct them, show superiority, ask for recognition, or give their own viewpoints unless they are leaders and it is their responsibility to do so.

2. The duty of the lecturer is to present the Teaching in such a way that he creates an interest in the audience to study the subject further, to read the book, or to do meditation.

3. Some lecturers praise their own ego, thinking that they are superior and that they have the right to humiliate others or to make them targets. Such an action will make people reject the Teaching.

4. Your lecture must radiate joy. You must be an example of humility, and you should encourage people to love the Teaching. To do this, try to have a positive attitude and do not think that you are there to teach. You are there to *present the Teaching*. The better you present the Teaching, the less your ego will find an opportunity to ask for praise.

5. Know that if you humiliate people with your attitude and create rejection, you become the enemy of the Teaching. You must just be a beautiful waitress or a handsome waiter who is dressed joyfully and neatly. Then serve your delicious dinner without making others become irritated, tense, or rejectful.

6. You have no right to take revenge on people while you lecture. Some egotistical lecturers think that they are superior to others, and they try to draw attention to themselves instead of to the Teaching. Once you fall into such a trap, it will be very difficult to save you. The best thing to do is to forget about yourself.

7. You should not come between the Teaching and the audience.

8. Never try to imitate the leader. He has different responsibilities and duties. You are a lecturer, so stay on your ground. When leadership is given to you, people will accept your guidance — but not while you are a lecturer.

9. Lecturing is given to you to make you more humble and more aware of your ignorance and fallacies. If such an awareness does not come to you after each lecture you give, you are in the wrong place and you are building vanity and ego.

10. Think! Who are you to attack people, to try and strengthen them, or to test them? Your duty is not to do anything *with* the audience but to present the Teaching joyfully to the people, with clarity and with beauty. It is the Teaching that will teach them, *not* you.

11. Know that you cannot lecture with your personality but only with your soul. The personality becomes occupied with the personality of others. The soul lights candles in the souls of others with his words.

The labors of each position are different. In a hospital, everyone works; but nurses have different duties from those who are interns, X-ray technicians, pharmacists, or surgeons.

The same holds true for an organized group. Not everybody has the same duty; not everyone teaches everything. Lecturers must know that they are on a path of promotion, and at every level or state they have special duties.

At the stage when the lecturer is involved in becoming integrated and a soul-infused personality, he has his limitations and *must only try to present the Teaching as it is given to him,* without trying to use the opportunity for personal considerations.

Humility must be experienced, especially at this stage, so that the ego is not allowed to have a chance to grow. In Buddhism, even the greatest disciples begin their lectures by saying, "And thus I heard . . . ."

You must try to present the Teaching only from that which you have read, listened to, and understood.

Watch and see if you are in your right role or if you are slipping onto the wrong path.

Notes:

1. Agni Yoga Society, *New Era Community*, para. 222.

41

Right Use of Time

Some employees have a tendency to appear occupied every minute, but do things halfway. For example they take a job, do not complete it, and start another job, another job, and another job, giving the impression that they are constantly doing things. It is true that they are working, but there is a great danger in the way they work. Soon you will find around you half-done jobs, and because of the time passed between these half done jobs, you will have difficulties starting and completing them as they were planned.

Some employees use such a method to make their bosses depend on them. Once a boss depends on the ways his employees work, he slowly becomes their slave and enters into a field of increasing problems.

Except in an emergency, every worker in the organization must start a job and finish it. It is a waste of time, energy, and focus to make workers change their job without making them finish the first job.

On certain occasions, when there is an unfinished job and another job is urgent, you can transfer an employee to

1. make the work move on in an emergency

2. give a rest to your employee

3. give an opportunity to another server

4. make people learn different jobs to be ready for emergencies

But the leader must be very careful of those who do half jobs. He must find out the reason why they are doing this.

Some of these workers create jobs for themselves that are nonessential. The leader must be careful not to let nonessential jobs flood the hours of a worker when he has essential work to do.

It is, of course, possible to give two to three jobs together to an employee to finish them, but one by one, not starting all at once and dragging them for months.

The leader must always be aware of the status of the jobs in the various offices.

True leadership must provide those conditions in the world in which worry, fear, and irritation will be ruled out. These are three sources which lead a group or a nation toward degeneration, sickness, and unhappiness. When these three factors are gradually eliminated, the health, prosperity, and happiness of a nation will increase.

A prosperous, healthy, and happy nation is a victorious nation, a nation in which a person can see cooperation, harmony, and creativity. As fear, irritation, and worry increase in a nation, that nation uses anti-survival methods to deal with other nations.

The true leaders of humanity must try by all possible means to create such conditions in which fear, irritation, and worry cannot breed in the world. This is the first responsibility of a leader.

In esoteric groups the same spirit must be demonstrated by the leaders. They must create those conditions in which fear, worry, and irritation will not breed. The words and actions of the leadership must not impose fear, worry, or irritation. This is the most crucial test because most leaderships are founded upon the above three negative conditions.

Most leaders continue their work by creating dependency — generating fear, worry, and irritation within the hearts of their followers — and thus they create a "followship" of unhealthy people around them. Most of the troubles and complications arising in groups are based on fear, worry, and irritation. People who are nourished by these three elements are those who use slander, malice, and treason against each other and against the leadership.

A healthy group is one that is not contaminated with fear, worry, and irritation. Groups can advance only through cooperation and in mutual trust. These two are pillars upon which the arch of success rests.

Fear, worry, and irritation make cooperation and mutual trust impossible. Future leaderships will find new ways of teaching and guidance which do not generate fear, worry, or irritation, ways in which no fear exists. Such a teaching will be charged with love, joy, light, and the spirit of peace and will be presented in such a way that it is readily accepted.

Leadership that manipulates fellow travelers with fear, worry, and irritation eventually misleads people who come for the Teaching, and in coming ages such a leader will pay a heavy taxation for his mistakes.

It is observed that when the government of a nation tries to control people with fear and imposes worry and irritation, that nation is lead to bankruptcy. Those nations which suffer economically and demonstrate a degenerate morality and health must know that these conditions were created by a leadership which imposed fear, worry, and irritation. Many nations have disappeared from the world because of these three evils.

A leader must follow a spiritual discipline to be able to create those conditions in which no fear, worry, and irritation exist.

The *first step* of discipline is to exercise right thinking, right speech, right action, and right relationship and to train fellow co-workers in the same virtues.

The *second step* in spiritual discipline is to activate and deepen one's faith and the power of withdrawal. This is the faith that Invisible Hosts will protect the leader's work because it is done for the glory of God and for the liberation and transformation of humanity. It is also withdrawal into the higher mental plane or into the Intuitional Plane, entering into peace, into the awareness that nothing bad happens to the Self, all earthly life is part of a great illusion, there are always opportunities to do things better, and all that happens will eventually be in favor of and for the glory of the One Self.

As the leader succeeds in withdrawing, he increases his efficiency to do things better within the field of his responsibilities.

The *third step* is renunciation, to be able to "let it go" and let the spiritual laws in the Universe take care of things.

The *fourth step* is to develop the awareness that all events are messengers of Good. They may be painful for the moment, but they hold great gifts for the future.

The *fifth step* of discipline is intense moments of prayer and surrender of oneself to the Almighty Presence.

With these five disciplines, the leader creates the best foundation for the ability to stand above fear, worry, and irritation and to inspire his fellow co-workers with the same spirit.

Sometimes people think that the moves of certain leaders are controlled by fear. It is very easy to translate into fear any wise move, cautious move, even a move of temporary retreat. But the leader knows how to play with opposing tides to cross the river with the least expenditure of energy.

The leader also knows how to temper the wills of his co-workers, for example:

1. He allows his co-workers to make a decision in a crucial moment.

2. He lets them fail, lose, or be defeated.

Once my father left me to be beaten by a boy of my own age. I was so angry that he did not come to my rescue. But because of that, six months later I was able to defend myself when the boy tried to beat me.

3. Often the leader consciously makes a few mistakes to see if his co-workers are awake or blind, if they are with him or will desert him.

4. The leader sometimes pretends that he does not see your mistakes or failures for two reasons:

    a. So as not to humiliate you or discourage you

    b. And to see if you are aware of your mistakes and failures

5. The leader may create problems and involve you with problems to see

    a. if you are capable of solving them

    b. if you are faint-hearted

    c. if you develop resentment against him

6. On certain occasions the leader points out your stupidity to see if you are identified with your stupidity or if you are detached from it.

7. The leader may desert you, ignore you, and abandon you to see if your faith toward the vision is strong enough to depend upon yourself.

There are many "games" that the leader plays with the intention to make you a strong, trustworthy, fearless, and intelligent leader.

42
Fear

Fear is the greatest enemy of man and humanity. Because of fear, humanity has fallen behind in its evolution.

It is very interesting to notice how people and leaders use fear to reach their goals, but every goal reached by fear is a heavy debt to be paid later.

The most important philosophy at this time will be a philosophy that frees people from fear and urges leaders not to use fear in any department of human endeavor.

It is through fear that dark forces gain ground and manipulate humanity in such a way that it traps itself in its own deeds.

Fear is a muddy current coming from the sphere of the dark lodge, and each ripple is a dark entity which contaminates life, brings hopelessness, depression, grief, pain, suffering, and death.

Fear spreads like a frost over seedlings and kills them. It freezes unfolding or developing labors, visions, and striving. Those who can defeat fear to a certain degree can, in that same degree, enter into light and into the path of progress.

Unfortunately, the muddy river of fear is flooding the human consciousness, and the agents of dark forces are spreading it everywhere.

On the other hand, the great leaders of humanity are pumping into the human consciousness hope, joy, future, and the possibilities of great success and victory.

All disciples must make efforts to join with the consciousness of their leaders and serve humanity. To do this, people must learn to control their mind and change their way of talking and relating with each other. A great change — perhaps the greatest — will come to humanity when fear is conquered and life is lived on the path of encouragement, optimism, help, hope, and joy.

In the future, great and talented people will come to earth to give us the philosophy of fearlessness upon which will be built the structure of the New Era.

The following exercise may help those who live in fear.

1. Sit relaxed.

2. Take one of your fears and see what can happen to you if your fear comes true. Then totally reverse the course of your fear, and defeat your "enemy" step by step with a glorious victory.

Most of the time fear is accumulated within our fabricated thoughtforms. To defeat such thoughtforms we need to create the opposites, then increase the opposing thoughts to such a degree that the gloomy thoughtforms are totally defeated and disintegrated.

3. In your visualization try to act with nobility, fearlessness, righteousness, and with a deep faith that all will be good for you and for others.

4. Exercise detachment from the part of your being that is under fear. This means affirm your True Self which has nothing to do with the fear.

5. Let loose your central energy source, and let it flood your being with joy.

Victory and defeat in the outer world are controlled within your mind. If you are victorious in your mind, you will be victorious in the outer life too.

Try to think fearlessly, victoriously, joyfully, and with beauty, and life will smile at you.

43

Leadership and Treason

A true leader must watch if his co-workers have seeds of jealousy, superiority, arrogance, showing off, a craving to be praised, or vanity. These are seeds which, when grown, stop the evolution of the person for ages and bring him lives full of suffering and dishonor. The leader must be extremely watchful that he does not promote such people nor draw them close to him.

Usually such people nourish their vices from the group magnetism and from the energy of the leader, lingering with the group and the leader.

The true leader must keep a close watch on them and not lose any opportunity to reveal to them their true nature. The greatest traitors are found in those people who were scolded and exposed by a leader in private or public about their vices. But the leader must take risks because if the snake is not eliminated when it is *small* it will be more difficult or even impossible to eliminate painlessly when in higher positions or in closer relationships with the group or the leader.

Humility is one of the greatest virtues. A humble man is a person who has no arrogance, false pride, showing off, craving for recognition, jealousy, or vanity.

Persons full of such weaknesses do almost everything possible to be in a position where people will praise them, flatter them, and make them feel superior to others, even superior to their Teachers.

Some of these people are possessed by dark ones and cause disturbances or shame to the movement they are in. Some of them inherit these weaknesses from the past. How these weaknesses form within them is not easy to explain. Many elements come together to form such weaknesses in a person.

For example, *vanity* is the accumulated result of lies said about yourself or about others.

Revenge is the accumulated result of past misdeeds during which one's conscience reproached him. We punish ourselves by developing vices from our past mistakes. *Showing off* is the result of accumulated failures in the past.

Sense of superiority is the result of an accumulation of moments in which flattery was bestowed upon us and false pride was pumped into us. *Arrogance* is the result of accumulated pain and suffering people caused us for their own interest. Such elements accumulate life after life, condense within our consciousness, and manifest as vices.

The duty of Teachers is to uproot such weeds from our nature. This work is risky and difficult and must be handled with extreme caution. These vices often have strong roots and are explosive materials that can cause great damage if the surgery is not done intelligently and at the right time.

Some group leaders watch until such vices mature and become visible to his true associates. Sometimes they use people with such vices to teach co-workers how they operate, and what their true nature is.

Sometimes they wait for a long time to make the owner of the vices see them and abhor them. Sometimes leaders wait until the contaminated one comes and confesses about his vices.

On such occasions the true leader uses the opportunity to make people realize a little more the path of danger they are walking on.

But also the leader knows how dangerous it is sometimes even to affirm vices that are confessed by a person. Often, poisonous serpents lying in the path reveal themselves when the confessor realizes that he has exposed himself. One must know that often their vices cannot be healed for a lifetime unless the victim cooperates wholeheartedly. This is why sometimes the leader must see but not make people know that he sees, listen to a confession and remain indifferent, realize the damage they are doing but silently try to repair the damage.

Sometimes the leader is even forced to use such persons in "the show," giving them the needed role to play. Sometimes the leader has total control over them and can stop them at any moment. Sometimes such a control turns dangerous because such people use servility to penetrate into deeper corners of the work. A leader must develop not only his power of observation but also his intuition. It is often his intuition that must help him to choose the way he should deal with them.

The Teacher says, "Promote people very slowly," because it is often very difficult to see the darkness that dwells in their hearts. Such people climb using knowledge of the faults of the leader or special ladders such as:

1. I am hurt. I will take revenge.

2. I need a victim to attack and forget my failures.

3. I cannot feel great unless I belittle someone.

4. I have a mission.

5. I must prove that I am "somebody" to those who "know" my worth.

6. I want to be the leader.

These ladders are used by traitors for imaginary or real positions. But the victim does not realize that the higher he goes, the deeper he will fall.

There are two kinds of devotion. One is selfless; the other is selfish.

Selfless devotion is the result of an ability to

1. see the group cause

2. believe in that cause

3. leave behind all self-interest

4. serve, identified with the cause, and work in cooperation with those who are similarly dedicated to the cause

5. demonstrate obedience to the law of sacrifice

Selfish devotion is a form of attachment to

1. introduce certain cleavages into the group

2. use the group for self-interest

3. satisfy jealousy and conceit

4. express vanity and to show off

5. take revenge on those he hates

6. expose a weakness existing in the leader or in the membership

7. lead the group to serve other, ulterior goals

Selfish devotees can be discovered by the following signs:

1. They show the spirit of servility and even try to make the leader believe that they are his protectors.

2. They use flattery and bribery.

3. Most of the time they show irritation, criticism, resentment, gossip, and make belittling remarks.

4. They arrange things behind the leader's back and often act as if they have his authority.

5. They act often in hate and anger, but suddenly change into a happy person. Be careful when this change comes. It is a trap.

6. They often try to make sexual offers to the leader or to the co-workers of the leader to find easy paths for their plans.

7. They act secretively, but on the other end they are widely open. They lecture about secrecy and "just between us," but they have other persons to whom your private life is reported directly.

Through these seven signs it will be easy to detect them. One of the main techniques to use when you have a doubt is to give them a few hard jobs at times of rest and pleasure and watch their maneuvers and attitudes. If they cannot take revenge on you for the hard labor you gave them, they take revenge on those whom you dearly love.

An experienced leader needs to go through a life filled with slander, malice, and treason to open his eyes. Once he is able to control situations caused by such vices, he will be promoted into more dangerous fields of labor where wolves walk in sheepskins.

Nature works very hard to help build a leader. Because the evolution of humanity is in the hands of leaders, they are needed not only on earth but primarily in the `Higher Worlds. Leaders are the co-workers of the Great Spirit. The leader must not be glamored by the social positions of the people nor by their titles or ranks nor by their family background. He must look and see if the light is shining in any person.

When the light is there, there will also be sincerity, selflessness, devotion, sacrificial will, joy, and enthusiasm.

These seven qualities are the rays of the light shining in the person.

An enlightened person is far superior to any scientist, professor, inventor, political or religious leader, or a wealthy man. One can be all of these, but his soul can still be in darkness. The leader will choose his co-workers from the ranks of such people, but, of course, he will also extend his compassion to those who are near him with wrong motives.

Some leaders are kept alert and vigilant only because of the traitors around them.

Index

A

Absolute
 and creation, 170
Achievement, 149
Actions
 kinds of, 171
Adepts
 and knowledge, 180
Ageless Wisdom
 on gifts, 245
 (See also Teaching)
Alcohol, 134
Alexander the Great, 131
Anger
 and letting go, 184
Appreciation
 of another, 101
 of others, 135
Archetype, 236
Archetypes
 and real leadership, 239
Argumentation, 24
Arguments
 and co-workers, 250
Arrogance, 306
Arrows, dark, 121
Art
 and confusion in, 96
Arts, 97
 and totalitarianism, 66
Arts, fine
 how distorted, 94
Ashram
 solemnity in, 257
Ashram, First Ray, 126
Ashrams, 106

Astral body
 and imagination, 188
Astral entities, 107
Astral plane
 and non-forgiveness, 187
 and vigilance, 107
 vices of, 180
Atlantian, 176
Atlantis, 67
Aura, 18, 107, 108, 120, 121, 257, 264
 and joy, 228
 and painful events, 184
 and renouncement, 154
 and revenge, 188
 disturbance in, 186
Aura
 magnetism in, 155
Aura, quality of
 and group work, 71
Aura readers, 53
Aura, webs in
 and bad expressions, 142

B

Balance, 51
 how achieved, 52
Balancing technique, 97
Battle
 and vigilance, 108
Beauty, 47, 95, 108, 111, 129, 150, 154, 205, 213, 231, 232
Beingness, 130, 131
Betrayal
 and leaders, 166
Board of Directors, 160
Bodies, three
 as results of, 204
Body of glory
 result of, 204
Brain clarity, 134

311

Buddha, 131, 237

C

Causal thinking, 133
Cause and effect
   and understanding, 290
Causeless Cause, 173
Center of leadership
   defined, 282
Centers
   and arrows, 121
Centers
   etheric, 186
Centers, various
   and experiences, 46
Central Spiritual Sun, 170
Certainty, 51, 87
   defined, 52
Chalice, 17, 46, 79
Children
   and labor, 164
   and vigilance, 108
Christ, 151, 237
Christ, message of, 190
Church
   example of emptiness, 37
Civilizations, failure of
   and humiliation, 100
Co-worker, 27
   and arguments with, 250
   and example with inventory, 159
   and files on work, 252
   and release of, 278
   and trust, 159
   failure, 28
Co-worker training, 28
Co-workers
   and ableness, 247
   and checking the work, 39
   and cultivating personality, 31
   and danger, 216

   and field of labor, 259
   and focus on labor, 277
   and indifference, 42
   and leadership, 275
   and orders, 33
   and personality, 208
   being watchful with, 257
   losing faith in, 193
   what to look for, 243
Common Good, 7
Communication
   and employees, 35
Compassion
   and repulsion, 74
Concentration, 51
   and non-forgiveness, 186
   how achieved, 52
Condemnation, self, 103
Conflict in group
   how handled, 160
Confusion
   and use in all fields, 90
   causes and effects, 87
   defined, 52
   how to get out of, 92
Conscience, 132
Conscious state
   and harmony, 172
Consciousness
   and machinery, 177
   expansion of, 175, 206
Consciousness
   burden on, 207
   continuity of, 108, 125
   expansion of, 133
Continuity, 283
Contraction
   as mental illness, 178
Control
   and service, 23
Conventions and retreats
   and confusion, 94

Cooperation
    pretended, 165
Cosmic energies
    and ideas, 237
Cosmic Evolution, 262
Cosmic Magnet, 106, 264
Courage, 134
Creativity, higher, 48
Creation, 173
Creative energies, 18
Creativity, 133, 208, 213
    and God, 12
    as inner success, 143
Creators, 173
Crime
    and losing faith, 141
Crime increase
    and leadership, 118
Crime rate
    increase of, 91
Criminals
    and education, 190
Crises
    and clearing vanities, 167
    and revealing motive, 275
Crown, jewels
    as eyes, 105
Crystallization
    results of, 179
Crystallizations
    defined, 81
Culture and civilization
    and experience, 47
    and totalitarianism, 66

D

Dance
    and confusion in, 96
    and order, 179
Dangers
    and how to handle, 215

Dangers
    kinds of, 216
Daring, 134
Dark forces, 47, 89
    and attack to group, 279
    and confusion, 94
    and joy, 228
    and tools of, 223
    and use of fear, 301
Debts
    payment of, 205
Defamation
    of leaders, 94
Defeats, self
    and lack of gratitude, 117
Democracy
    and leadership, 114
    and voting, 115
    true sense of, 221
Democracy, pseudo, 118, 119
Depression, 21
    and confusion, 92
    and fanaticism, 228
Detachment
    and group life, 78
    and repulsion, 75
Devadatta, 15
Devotion
    selfless and selfish, 308
Dialogues
    purposes for, 83
Dictatorship
    how to avoid, 122
Disciple
    and forgiveness, 183
Disciple, duties of
    and greatness, 141
Discipleship
    defined, 285
Discipleship obstacles
    and personal interests, 84

Discipline
   and tests for candidates, 166
Discrimination, 53, 74
   and nations, 209
Dishonesty
   effects of, 116
Divine carelessness, 196
Divine indifference, 73, 201
Divorce, 92
Dominating others, 206
Donated items
   how to handle, 159
Doubt
   causes for, 88
Drugs, 134
Duties
   spreading of, 165
Dweller on Threshold, 121, 122

E

Economics, 97
Education, 90, 97, 220
   and leadership, 200
   and standards, 118
   and totalitarianism, 66
   for real democracy, 122
Educational process
   and standards, 118
Ego, 211, 217
   and Leadership, 23
   and repulsion, 75
   and workers, 41
Ego and Love, 18
Elementals, 207
   and self respect, 103
Emotional forgiveness, 188
Emotions
   and life, 180
Employees
   and incomplete work, 295
   and mistakes, 36

Emptiness, 204
Endurance, 254
Enemies
   and future of nations, 206
Enemy, transformed
   and greatness, 143
Energy
   how leaked, 207
Enthusiasm, 134
Etheric body
   and vices, 122
Evil
   vigilance of, 109
Evolution
   and Laws of Nature, 203
   as awakening, 111
   defined, 170
Evolution
   conscious, 139
Evolution, path of
   and forgiveness, 187
Exercise:
   To release fear, 302
Experience, 45
Expressions for failure, 142
Eye, Watching, 140

F

Failure, 22
   and insignificance, 141
Failure
   fear of, 213
Failure thoughtforms
   how destroyed, 142
Failures, 139
   and condemnation, 103
Failures, past
   and success, 48
Faintheartedness, 158
Faith, 206
Faith, losing, 144

Fame, 37
Fanaticism, 14, 24, 122, 178, 208, 228
Fear, 296, 301
   and candidate, 166
   and confusion, 91
   and decision-making, 47
   as tool, 89
Fearlessness, 134, 218
   and repulsion, 75
Flattery, 101
Forgiveness, 183
Freedom, 95, 108, 111, 130, 150, 154, 205, 213, 231, 232
   defined, 177
Freedom, personal
   lack of, 118
Freedom, real
   and innate greatness, 143
Freeways of life, 165
Future
   how changed, 151

G

Galactic Logoi, 170
Gardens
   of true Servers, 263
Glamor, 121
Glamors, 47
   and renunciation, 154
   defined, 223
Glandular function
   and forgiveness, 185
Goals, 88
God
   how defined, 11
God
   relation with, 207
Gods, imperfect, 172
Golden Age
   defined, 108

Goodness, 47, 95, 108, 111, 130, 150, 154, 205, 213, 231, 232
Gossip
   how to handle, 266
Gratitude, 116
Great One
   result of contact with, 102
Great Ones
   and guidance, 139
   and your greatness, 139
   methods of, 150
Greatness
   striving toward, 102
Greed, 24, 180
Group
   and vices of members, 305
   defined, 7
Group Consciousness, 40
Group formation
   and having faith, 194
   and repulsion, 77
Group health
   and qualities of leadership, 297
Group life
   and what to repulse, 72
Group members
   and repulsion, 71
   and responsibility, 160
   and tension, 208
   and trustworthiness, 160
Group membership
   and Teaching, 157
Group work
   and being a soul, 75
Groups
   and attacks to, 157
Growth
   and expansion of horizon, 208
Guardian
   and vigilance, 108

Guidance, inner, 113
  defined, 125

H

Harmlessness, 206
Hatred, 180, 204
Health
  and forgiveness, 185
Health, mental, 51
Heart, 106
Heart of Sun, 70
Hearts
  and love of labor, 163
Hero
  defined, 140
Heroes, 137
Heroes
  and education, 123
Hiawatha, 120
Hierarchies, Divine, 173
Hierarchy, 42, 130, 134
  and dangers, 218
  and guidance, 126
  and repulsion, 77
Higher Powers, 213
Higher Worlds, 9, 17, 197, 220, 309
  contact with, 82
Hope, 228
Human being
  as a flow, 179
Humiliation technique, 97
Humility, 134
  and lecturing, 293
  defined, 305
  exaggerated, 14
Hypnotism, self, 103

I

Ideas
  and leaders, 235

Ideas, true
  defined, 238
Identity
  how built, 17
Illusion, 121
Illusions, 47, 223
Image, self
  and identity, 104
Imagination, 188
  and reason, 180
Imperil, 185
Indifference, 42
Inertia, 255
Initiation, Fourth, 79
Initiation, path of
  and forgiveness, 187
Inner Watch, 113, 129, 132
  and contact with, 200
Inspiration
  and Great Ones, 150
Insulation
  for leader, 199
Integrity, 222
  defined, 223
Intuition, 95
  and repulsion, 74
  defined, 50
Intuitional Plane, 49, 109
  and vigilance, 108
Irritation, 296

J

Jealousy, 24, 180
Jesus
  and Herod, 149
  and miracles, 149
Joy, 95, 108, 111, 130, 150, 154, 205, 213, 231, 232
  and training, 166
  in letters and relations, 227
Joy in labor, 163

Judas, 15
Judgment
   sound, 271
Justice
   defined, 189

K

Karma, 129, 132, 150, 162, 172, 196, 197, 206
   and non-forgiveness, 188
   and success, 205
   and young leaders, 262
   as the cause, 170
   speed of, 120
Karmic Lords, 149
Karmic problems
   how solved, 278
Knowledge
   increase of, 180
Knowledge
   as acid, 206
Krishna, 237

L

Labor, love of
   and leadership, 163
Ladders
   and Teaching, 170
Language
   psychological, 288
Language, use of
   and leader, 287
Law
   and will, 63
   defined, 203
   three kinds of, 76
   (See also Chapter 12)
Law of Attraction, 123, 282
Law of Building the Bridge, 123
Law of Destroying Angel, 79
Law of Economy, 123

Law of Future, 123
Law of Incarnation, 123
Law of Integrity, 223
Law of Karma, 22, 74, 123, 147, 173, 185, 190
   (See also Karma)
Law of Life
   and doing best, 207
Law of Reincarnation, 197
Law of Repulsion, 69
Law of Synthesis, 78, 123
Law of Transmutation, 79
Law of Unity, 132
Laws
   and Great Ones, 66
Laws
   various, 207
Laws of Nature, 123
   and vices, 155
   how best used, 151, 203
Leader
   and advice giving, 255
   and anxieties, 199
   and dealing with limitations, 196
   and dealing with wounds, 255
   and defeats, 21
   and depending on others, 244
   and election, 114
   and failure, 243
   and future, 6
   and giving guidance, 255, 258
   and group's association, 244
   and handling co-workers, 248
   and higher values, 200
   and Higher Worlds, 119
   and ideal, 22
   and indifference, 41
   and insulation, 199
   and length of influence, 233
   and link to Higher Worlds, 115
   and mistakes of co-workers, 251
   and need to meditate, 199

and path of ascent, 284
and problem solving, 254
and purpose, 254
and recovery, 256
and relation to past leaders, 283
and retreat/attack, 276
and sacrificing co-workers, 278
and self humiliation, 21
and spiritual discipline steps, 297
and "spiritual fever", 14
and standards, 243
and status of jobs, 296
and Subtle Worlds, 114
and Teaching, 157
and tempering wills of others, 298
and true responsibility, 197
and trust, 159
and use of language, 287
and vices of co-workers, 305
and weaknesses, 247
and wounds, 43
as a thinker, 10
as center, 281
as example, 115
as link, 231
as serving souls of others, 231
as spiritual teacher, 6
how to choose, 221
how to train, 249
qualities to look for, 249
Leader
 building of, 309
Leader and followers
 and involutionary forces, 197
Leader and group
 as etheric body, 195
Leader, efficiency of
 and co-workers, 275
Leader, Great
 and things not done, 113

Leader, real
 and standards, 117
Leader, relating with
 and expectation, 37
Leader to be
 signs of, 42
Leader, true
 and attitude toward achievement, 253
 and respect to leaders, 283
 and sense of value, 252
Leader, voted for
 and degeneration, 117
Leaders
 and core values, 5
 and departments of life, 7
 and training co-workers, 282
 and various consultants, 126
 defamation of, 94
 how selected, 124
 qualities needed, 5
Leaders by vote
 and responsibility, 120
Leaders, contemporary
 and relation with dangers, 215
Leaders, Elder, 261
Leader's field
 as wild horse, 43
Leader's intention
 and warriors, 218
Leaders, real
 why rejected, 118
Leaders, true
 and human salvation, 167
Leaders, young
 and Elders, 262
Leadership
 and actualization of vision, 260
 and contradiction, 195
 and cultivating healthy conditions, 297
 and dangers, 215

and fruit of labor, 232
and future leaders, 260
and glamors and vanities, 155
and harmlessness, 121
and ideas, 235
and inner guidance, 113
and integrity, 222
and losing faith, 193
and motive, 241
and non compromise, 197
and personality failures, 10
and personality vehicles, 9
and political interests, 232
and pressures, 27
and principles, 6
and psychic energy, 129
and quality workers, 247
and records of work, 229
and role of women, 124
and security, 116
and self-confidence development, 129
and selflessness, 213
and traps, 224
and use of fear, 301
and viewpoints, 222
and virtues of co-workers, 219
and withdrawal, 156
as an interest, 156
as continuity, 43
as creating freedom, 122
as influence, 231
defined, 6
education for, 123
foundations, 116
guidelines to, 254
how learned, 9
how to lead, 220
in various countries, 125
Leadership
enemies of, 211

Leadership applicants
training of, 162
Leadership candidates
tests for, 163
Leadership, dishonest
and effect on people, 116
Leadership duties
and dangers, 218
Leadership, false
and results of, 238
Leadership group
handling conflict, 160
Leadership, new
and crystallization, 169
Leadership power
and past experiences, 15
Leadership responsibility
and heroes, 137
Leadership, strong
and arrows, 121
Leadership training, 276
and infinity, 164
and motives, 164
Lecturer
and cultural differences, 288
Lecturers
guidelines for, 291
Lemurian, 176
Letters
art of, 225
Light, 205
Listening, 288
Literature
and lasting influence, 291
Logic
defined, 49
Logic and reasoning
path of growth, 49
Loneliness, 284
Love
and building identity, 17
and leadership, 198

Love and respect, 207

M

Manifestation, 169
Manipulators, 218
Mantram of Self, 103
Marijuana, 90
Matter
   as used in evolution, 170
Maya, 121
Meditation, 13, 51, 199, 290
   and glamors, 143
   creative, 25
   how confused, 95
Meditation, reflective
   and laws of Nature, 204
Meditation report, 55
Men
   three types of, 9
Mental body
   abscesses in, 208
Mental illness
   and contraction, 178
Mental plane
   and vigilance, 107
Mind, 106
Ministers, Exterior and Interior, 124
Miracles
   renouncement of, 147
Money in group
   care for, 160
Moral downfall
   and leadership, 118
Moral standards, 90
Moses, 118, 131
Motive
   and co-worker, 275
   and leadership, 241
Motive, right
   and clearing confusion, 89

Musical field
   and confusion, 95
Mystics
   and renunciation, 153

N

Nadis, 185
Nathan, prophet, 131
National bankruptcy
   and imposition, 297
Nationalism, 206
Nation's prosperity, 296
Nature
   and challenge to greatness, 138
   and greatness, 144
   and relation to man, 84
Nature, as one, 206
New Era
   and fearlessness, 302
News media
   and fear, 90
Nirvani, 282
Nosiness, 25

O

Obedience
   and use of power, 100
Observation, 105, 143
Observation,
   art of, 133
Oceans, 138
Optimism
   and letters, 226
Orderliness, 175
   and Cosmos, 177
Organization
   spiral quality, 177
Organizations
   as organism, 175

P

Parables
  as ladders, 289
Past life readers, 53
Path, 51
  and group work, 71
Patience, 254
Perfection
  false, 187
Perfection, path of, 85
Perseverance, 208
Personality
  and control of, 199
  and Leadership, 10
  how built, 32
  treasures, 26
Personality aspect
  and laws, 76
Philosophy
  and totalitarianism, 66
Pity, 74
Plan, 42, 73, 74, 84, 105, 126, 133, 282
  and group work, 71
Planning
  and voice of experience, 47
Plato, 86
  and education, 126
Political ideology, 177
Political powers
  and exploitation, 176
Political weapons, 180
Politics, 90, 97
  and totalitarianism, 66
Pollution, 114
Power, 221
  and law, 64
Power, spiritual, 131
Prayer, 106
  requests, 162
Pressures, various
  as training, 27
Progress, 149
  and greatness, 138
  hindrance to, 180
Progressive life, 177
Promotion, 43
Promotion of traitors
  ladders used, 307
Psychic Energy, 130
Psychic energy, 129, 132, 134
  and imperil, 185
  and letters, 225
Psychic fields
  and confusion, 93
Psychic influences
  and students, 53
Psychic, lower
  and creating confusion, 94
Psychics, lower, 217
  and leaders, 126
Purpose, 74, 84, 133, 282
Purpose, Cosmic, 135

R

Racism, 206
Radiation, 173
Ray, First
  and group work, 70
  and higher expression, 78
  and indifference, 73
Ray qualities, 32
Rays
  and group affiliation, 70
Rays, Seven
  and Law of Repulsion, 72
Reactions from others
  reason for, 200
Reality
  and relation to certainty, 88
  defined, 236

Reasoning
  defined, 49
Rejection
  and group life, 71
Religion, 90, 97, 177
  and totalitarianism, 67
Renunciation, 153
Repulsion
  intent of, 77
Respect, 37
Respect, self, 103
Responsibility
  and leadership, 119
Revenge, 188, 306
Righteousness, 47, 95, 108, 111, 116, 130, 150, 154, 205, 213, 231, 232
Rishis, Seven, 73

S

School
  as human being, 11
Science, 97
Science of Impression, 150
Secretary
  and meditation courses, 54
Security
  and dangers, 219
Self, 53
  and show-off, 211
Self
  greatness in, 139
Self, All, 135
Self, One, 85, 135, 213, 236
Self, Real, 102
Self, True, 111, 134, 207, 302
Self-actualization, 140
Self-confidence, 129
Self-determination, 135
Self-forgetfulness, 73
Self-interest, 207

Self-perfection, 85
Self-respect, 17
Selfishness, 178
Selflessness, 208, 213
Sensitivity, 95
Service
  and faith, 263
  and finding motive, 242
Service
  sacrificial, 134
Service, law of, 71
Sex
  and Leadership, 24
Sharing, 207
Show-off, 211
Showing off, 306
Socrates, 131
Solar Angel, 79
  as an ideal, 102
Solar Heart, 76
Solar Laws, 172
Solar Logos, 172
Solemnity, 134, 257
Solomon, King
  quote from proverbs, 109
Soul, 53
  and achievement, 149
  and Cosmic Ideas, 237
  and leader, 221
Soul aspect
  and laws, 76
Soul contact
  and discrimination, 74
Soul energy
  flow of, 25
Soul, energy from
  and certainty, 96
Soul guidance
  and nosiness, 26
Soul, human, 135, 236, 282
  and divine heritage, 139
  and greater souls, 12

Index 323

and indifference, 72
and logic, 50
and maya, 122
and role in lecturing, 293
and service, 71
and vigilance, 107, 108
emancipation, 79
steps of evolution, 283
Soul, killing of, 141
Soul of student, 57
Soul, service of
and hindrances, 25
Soul-infusion, 32
Space, fires of, 237
Space, Infinite, 264
Speech
and stories, 290
Speech
control of, 254
metaphorical, 291
Spirit, 106
Spirit aspect
and laws, 76
Spiritual fever
defined, 12
Spiritual progress, 151
Spiritual Triad, 282
Spiritual values
and renunciation, 153
Spiritual visions
and vanities, 156
Spirituality, 190
defined, 15
Staff, 131
Standards
how to educate for, 118
Stars, 138
Stock market
and confusion, 90
Story:
By Nasrudin
Keeping Teaching whole, 83

Of Buddhist parable
using stories in lecturing, 289
Of Christ and forgiveness, 183
Of co-worker tests, 27
Of engineer
using right language, 288
Of girl and inferiority
developing confidence, 101
Of leader and photo
humility, 232
Of leader and piano
problems with gifts, 245
Of Nasrudin's wife
changing the Teaching, 85
Of neighbor and opium
use of humiliation, 99
Of new leader
reverence to previous leader, 284
Of pharmacist
developing potentials, 36
Of preparing schedule, 179
Of psychic
creating confusion, 93
Of river flow
labor and co-workers, 278
Of T.S. and book
showing-off, 212
Of T.S. and friend
contraction, 178
Of T.S. and Teacher
balanced judgment, 272
Of T.S. and trench
balancing extremes, 272
Of T.S. in restaurant
humiliation of woman, 98
Of teacher & school
building character, 10
Of teacher and Chalice
value of co-workers, 253
Of three sticks
staying awake, 111

Of wave dream
  love, 18
Straight knowledge, 95
Striving
  power of, 238
Students
  as gifts, 59
Subconscious mind
  and confusion, 91
Subtle Worlds
  and leader, 113
Success
  and higher powers, 213
  and tasks, 213
  how measured, 263
Success
  inner and outer, 142
  real source of, 151
Suicide, 92
Sun, levels of
  and laws, 76
Superiority sense, 306
Synthesis, 7, 130

T

Talents, 25
  why recognized, 260
Teacher, 113, 201, 212, 272, 273
  and balancing, 97
  and greatness, 140
  and lecturing with soul, 293
  and responsibility, 137
Teacher, real
  and unworthy students, 85
Teacher, role of, 53
Teacher, spiritual
  defined, 7
Teachers, 306
Teachers, false, 217
Teaching, 105, 158
  about manifestation, 169
  and crystallization, 81
  and leader, 157, 220
  and meditation courses, 57
  and self-interest, 84
  and Source, 86
  and use for personal benefit, 84
  how rejected, 94
  how to present, 291
  how to use, 82
Teaching, enemies of
  and controlling Teacher, 201
Teaching, level of
  and relating to us, 85
Teaching of the Future, 83
Teachings
  and ideas, 237
Telepathy, 150
Telephone rules, 265
Tension
  and face of danger, 216
Tests for leader candidates
  and motives, 165
Thinking
  process of, 10
Thinking
  goal of, 207
Thought, destructive
  and vigilance, 107
Thought, good
  and healing, 121
Thoughtform, 10, 238
  painful, 184
Thoughts
  and Law of Repulsion, 78
Totalitarian power
  and use of confusion, 93
Totalitarianism, 65, 175
  defined, 119
Traitors
  and mistakes, 252
Transpersonal Self, 102
Treason, 276

Trust
    and success, 208
Tumors
    and contraction, 178

U

United Nations, 156
Unity, 108, 111, 130
Universal forces
    and labor, 264

V

Value
    how realized, 206
Values
    abstract and material, 271
Vanity, 23, 130, 134, 211, 217, 306
    and candidates, 166
    and group members, 157
    and renunciation, 154
Vices
    how accumulated, 306
Victory, 302
    and internal conflict, 273
Vigilance, 105
    how to develop, 109
Virtue
    as actualized, 208
Virtues, 25
    and certainty, 53
    and glamors, 156
    and octaves, 74
Vision, 207
    and work of leaders, 261
Visualization
    and subjective experience, 48

W

Warrior, 108

Warriors, 219
Warriors of Future
    qualities of, 219
Watchfulness, 105
Waterfalls, 138
Will
    and law, 63
Will
    development of, 264
Willpower, 17, 111
Wisdom, 221
Women
    and departments of leadership, 124
    as faculty, 125
    how controlled, 97
    how freed, 98
Worry, 296
Worship
    freedom of, 209
Worthlessness
    and losing faith, 144

Bibliographic References

Agni Yoga Society. New York: Agni Yoga Society.
>*Fiery World*, Vol. III, 1948.
>*New Era Community*, 1951.

Bailey, Alice A. New York: Lucis Publishing Co.
>*A Treatise on Cosmic Fire*, 1977.

Lamsa, George M., trans. Nashville, TN: Holman Bible Publishers.
>*New Testament*, 1968.

Saraydarian, Torkom. Sedona, AZ: Aquarian Educational Group.

>*The Bhagavad Gita*, 1974.
>*Cosmos in Man*, 1983.
>*Hiawatha and the Great Peace,* 1984.
>*The Psyche and Psychism*, 2 vols., 1981.

Saraydarian, Torkom. Cave Creek, AZ: T.S.G. Publishing Foundation, Inc.

>*The Ageless Wisdom*, 1990.
>*Breakthrough to Higher Psychism*, 1990.
>*Other Worlds*, 1991.
>*The Mystery of Self-Image*, 1993.
>*The Sense of Responsibility in Society*, 1989.
>Video — *"The Seven Rays Interpreted"*, 1992.

About the Author

The *Leadership Series* is based on Torkom Saraydarian's life experiences as a leader, teacher, author, and musician.

The author's books have been used all over the world as sources of guidance and inspiration to live a life based on the teachings of the Ageless Wisdom. Some of the books have been translated into other languages, including Armenian, German, Dutch, Danish, Portuguese, French, Spanish, Italian, Greek, Yugoslavian, and Swedish. He holds lectures and seminars in the United States as well as in other parts of the world.

Torkom Saraydarian's entire life has been a zealous effort to help people live healthy, joyous, and successful lives. He has spread this message of love and true vision tirelessly throughout his life.

From early boyhood the author learned first-hand from teachers of the Ageless Wisdom. He has studied widely in world religions and philosophies. He is in addition an accomplished pianist, violinist, and cellist and plays many other instruments as well. His books, lectures, seminars, and music are inspiring and offer a true insight into the beauty of the Ageless Wisdom.

Other Books by Torkom Saraydarian

The Ageless Wisdom
The Bhagavad Gita
Breakthrough to Higher Psychism
Buddha Sutra — A Dialogue with the Glorious One
Challenge for Discipleship
Christ, The Avatar of Sacrificial Love
A Commentary on Psychic Energy
Cosmic Shocks
Cosmos in Man
Dialogue with Christ
Dynamics of Success
Flame of Beauty, Culture, Love, Joy
The Flame of the Heart
Hiawatha and the Great Peace
The Hidden Glory of the Inner Man
I Was
Joy and Healing
Leadership Vol. I
Legend of Shamballa
The Mysteries of Willpower
New Dimensions in Healing
Olympus World Report...The Year 3000
One Hundred Names of God
Other Worlds
The Psyche and Psychism
The Psychology of Cooperation and Group Consciousness
The Purpose of Life
The Science of Becoming Oneself

The Science of Meditation
The Sense of Responsibility in Society
Thought and the Glory of Thinking
Sex, Family, and the Woman in Society
The Solar Angel
Spring of Prosperity
Spiritual Regeneration
The Subconscious Mind and the Chalice
Symphony of the Zodiac
Talks on Agni
Triangles of Fire
Unusual Court
Wisdom From My Heart
Woman, Torch of the Future
The Year 2000 & After

Booklets

A Daily Discipline of Worship
Cornerstones of Health
Earthquakes and Disasters — What the Ageless Wisdom Tells Us
Fiery Carriage and Drugs
Five Great Mantrams of the New Age
Hierarchy and the Plan
Mental Exercises
Nachiketas
New Beginnings
Practical Spirituality
The Psychology of Cooperation
Questioning Traveler and Karma
Saint Sergius
Synthesis
Torchbearers

Booklets (Excerpts and Compilations)

Angels and Devas
Building Family Unity
Courage
First Steps Toward Freedom
Irritation — The Destructive Fire
Responsibility
Responsibility and Business
Responsibilities of Fathers
Responsibilities of Mothers
Success
What to Look for in the Heart of Your Partner

Videos

The Seven Rays Interpreted
Lecture Videos by Author

Next Release: *Leadership - Volume III*

For an updated list of publications, please contact T.S.G. Publishing Foundation, Inc.

Ordering Information

Write to the publisher for additional information regarding:

— Free catalog of author's books and music tapes
— Lecture tapes and videos — complete list available
— Placement on mailing list
— New releases
— A free copy of our newsletter *Outreach*

Additional copies of ***Leadership - Volume II***

U.S.$25.00 (Hardcover)
U.S.$20.00 (Softcover)

Postage within U.S.A. - $5.00
Plus applicable state sales tax
International postage: contact us for rates

T.S.G. Publishing Foundation, Inc.
P. O. Box 7068
Cave Creek, AZ 85331-7068
United States of America

TEL: (602) 502-1909
FAX: (602) 502-0713
EMAIL: TSGPUB@GNN.COM

T.S.G. Publishing Foundation, Inc. is a non-profit, tax exempt organization.

Our purpose is to be a pathway for self-transformation. We offer books, audio and video tapes, classes and seminars, and home study courses based on the core values and higher principles of the Ageless Wisdom.

These fine books have been published by the generous donations of the students of the Ageless Wisdom.

Your tax deductible contributions will help us continue publishing and growing.

Our gratitude to all.